URSULA LE GUIN'S EARTHSEA

Figure 1 Map of Earthsea, by permission of the Ursula K. Le Guin Children's Trust.

The Whale Isles

Lef

North Enwas
South Enwas

Bereswek

Komokome

Chemish

Sort

The Allernots

Ferrins

The North Reach

leshun
Sea

The Andrades

Orandra

The North Spear
The Jaws
The Teeth

Andrad

Oranéa

Gont

Gont Port
Kimesor
Skull Port

Ferregal

d Sea

of Éa

Ebéa

Spevy

Barnisk

The Kargad Lands

Nesheri
Hur-at-Hur

Torheven

Eskel

The Torikles

Atnini

Onwabeth

Atuan

Tenal

Karego-At

Enlad Ris
Mt. Onn
Enlad

Kembermouth

Eskel

Way

The Hands

Great
Port

Felkway
Skullgate

Waymarch

Vemish

Sattins

Freshwater

Venway

Vor

Ebavnor
Straits

Perilane
Outer
Innran

Ilien

The East Reach

Koppish

Sneg
Far
Toly

Vissti
Leng

Pendor

Toky

Iffish

Pody Port Geese
The Closed Sea

Bars of Uoy

Korp
Help
Insmer

Ranery

Ably

Namien

Kopp
Askt

Sewl

Pala-meny

Soders

The
Sellets

Misk
Set
Pugnel

Gale

Wasny

Pelimer

Gosk

Kornay

Astowell

The Great South Shoals

Isle of the
Ear

Miles

25 50   100   200   300

©2022 Ursula K. Le Guin Literary Trust

My Reading

JOHN PLOTZ

URSULA LE GUIN'S EARTHSEA

OXFORD
UNIVERSITY PRESS

Great Clarendon Street, Oxford, OX2 6DP,
United Kingdom

Oxford University Press is a department of the University of Oxford.
It furthers the University's objective of excellence in research, scholarship,
and education by publishing worldwide. Oxford is a registered trade mark of
Oxford University Press in the UK and in certain other countries

Published in the United States of America by Oxford University Press
198 Madison Avenue, New York, NY 10016, United States of America

British Library Cataloguing in Publication Data
Data available

Library of Congress Control Number: 2022948230

ISBN 978-0-19-284788-1

DOI: 10.1093/oso/9780192847881.001.0001

Printed and bound by
CPI Group (UK) Ltd, Croydon, CR0 4YY

SERIES INTRODUCTION

This series is built on a simple presupposition: that it helps to have a book recommended and discussed by someone who cares for it. Books are not purely self-sufficient: they need people and they need to get to what is personal within them.

The people we have been seeking as contributors to *My Reading* are readers who are also writers: novelists and poets; literary critics, outside as well as inside universities, but also thinkers from other disciplines—philosophy, psychology, science, theology, and sociology—beside the literary; and, not least of all, intense readers whose first profession is not writing itself but, for example, medicine, or law, or a non-verbal form of art. Of all of them we have asked: What books or authors feel as though they are deeply *yours*, influencing or challenging your life and work, most deserving of rescue and attention, or demanding of feeling and use?

What is it like to love this book? What is it like to have a thought or idea or doubt or memory, not cold and in abstract, but live in the very act of reading? What is it like to feel, long after, that this writer is a vital part of your life? We ask our authors to respond to such bold questions by writing not conventionally but personally—whatever "personal" might mean, whatever form or style it might take, for them as individuals. This does not mean overt confession at the expense of a chosen book or author; but nor should our writers be afraid of making autobiographical connections. What was wanted was whatever made for their own hardest thinking in careful relation to quoted sources and specifics. The work was to go on in the taut and resonant space between these readers and their chosen books. And the interest within that area begins precisely when it is no longer clear how much is coming from the text and how much is coming from its readers—where that distinction is no longer easily tenable because neither is sacrificed to the other. That would show what reading meant at its most serious and how it might have relation to an individual life.

Out of what we hope will be an ongoing variety of books and readers, *My Reading* offers personal models of what it is like to care about particular authors, to recreate through specific examples imaginative versions of what those authors and works represent, and to show their effect upon a reader's own thinking and development.

ANNE CHENG

PHILIP DAVIS

JACQUELINE NORTON

MARINA WARNER

MICHAEL WOOD

For my Friends

Think where man's glory most begins and ends,
And say my glory was I had such friends.

(W. B. Yeats, "The Municipal Gallery Revisited")

ACKNOWLEDGMENTS

Earthsea, used with permission, is a registered trademark of The Ursula K. Le Guin Children's Trust—which is also gratefully acknowledged for use of the copyrighted Map of Earthsea. The dragon preceding Chapter 1 is from Katsushika Hokusai's *Picture Book on Heroes of China and Japan* (1850) from the Metropolitan Museum Collection Open Access program. The dragon preceding Chapter 2 is Leonardo Da Vinci's "A Design for a Dragon Costume" (*c*.1517–18) from the Royal Collection (RCIN 912369). The dragon overlaid with human faces preceding Chapter 3, Michelangelo's "Dragon and Other Sketches" (*c*.1520–30; item 15190) is © Ashmolean Museum, University of Oxford. The dragon preceding Chapter 4 is an instance of "textual micrography" drawn from the British Library's Yonah Pentateuch (Add MSS 21160; *c*.1300–99). Acknowledgments go to the Alexander Turnbull Library of Wellington New Zealand for the cover image: William Fox, "Opara" (Jan 1868; Ref: WC-091).

My family, unreservedly beloved, is the hidden inspiration for this book. I started dreaming about Earthsea thanks to my parents Paul and Judith. They let me make my way to the library alone, and never questioned what followed. Along with them my brother David showed me what makes family, so I guess I have to forgive him for preferring fact to fantasy. If my childhood was fortunate, it pales in comparison to the adulthood I have spent and plan to go on spending with Lisa Soltani, who is everything to me. For two decades, that life was wrapped around our children Alan and Daria, who are beyond everything, including comparison. Now that they have left us, like the comets they are, we count the days until they spin by again.

Ursula Le Guin spent a lifetime exploring solidarity, camaraderie, and trustworthy friendship. From her I learned to lean on others in times of need and to be there when their turn came to lean. There is no other way to stand up straight. Four true friends—Alex Star, Ivan Kreilkamp, Leah Price, and Sean McCann—read this entire book in draft; their comments, asides, interjections, and jibes improved it immensely. The gratitude I feel for what Alex, Ivan, Leah, and Sean did and the trust I put in their counsel is a product of their generosity not over years but over decades.

So let those four names stand for all those other friends I won't name here. You know who you are. You know that I count on you and turn to you, and do my best to show up for you. But you may have no idea what that means to me, no idea of what flows below the banter. This book is dedicated to you, for what you've taught me about solidarity and about love.

CONTENTS

LIST OF ILLUSTRATIONS

INTRODUCTION

Reading and Rereading Le Guin

Fullness is a fine thing, but emptiness is the secret of it.[1]

Love

Whati makes readers fall in love? I can only speak for one childhood—and one adulthood—spent reading Le Guin, but I would bet my last nickel there are thousands of us out there. It had me from the start:

> The island of Gont, a single mountain that lifts its peak a mile above the storm-racked Northeast Sea, is a land famous for wizards. From the towns in its high valleys and the ports on its dark narrow bays many a Gontishman has gone forth to serve the Lords of the Archipelago in their cities as wizard or mage, or, looking for adventure, to wander working magic from isle to isle of all Earthsea. Of these some say the greatest, and surely the greatest voyager, was the man called Sparrowhawk, who in his day became both dragonlord and Archmage. His life is told of in the Deed of Ged and in many songs, but this is a tale of the time before his fame, before the songs were made.[2]

Day, weeks, and months went by when half of me was walking to school, the other half wandering Gont's high valleys. I was sleeping in my ordinary 1970's Washington DC bedroom—and on a boat tossed by the storm-racked Northeast Sea.

J. R. R Tolkien—a leading theorist of fantasy, among other things—praises the writer's godlike power to suspend all awareness of the world beyond the printed page. According to him, when things go right:

> the story-maker proves a successful "subcreator." He makes a Secondary World which your mind can enter. Inside it, what he relates is "true"; it accords with the laws of that world. You therefore believe it while you are, as it were, inside. The moment disbelief arises, the spell is broken; the magic, or the art, has failed.[3]

That is not quite how Le Guin operates. Her stories, her characters, even her sentences leave her readers in a state of half magic. Reading the Earthsea books, I find myself both inside the spell and outside it. That double power, the capacity to *semi*-detach her readers from their ordinary world, finds an echo in the nature of Earthsea itself. It is a land both of dragon-taming wizardry and of goatherds huddled with their goats, caught in a passing shower. Magic, meet humdrum prose. The doubleness is all. I wrote a whole scholarly book about this kind of doubleness, but I saved its most brilliant practitioner for a book all her own.[4]

In a sense this is a deeply personal book, about how one professor of Victorian literature regained his childhood love of fantasy. It begins, though, as an extended response to the six works of fantasy that Le Guin wrote about the sprawling archipelago called Earthsea, my childhood half-residence. More than any other series I know, Le Guin's Earthsea holds the secret to fantasy's present-day appeal—and its radical political potential.

Tolkien and Lloyd Alexander knew how to conquer evil; Beverly Cleary and Louise Fitzhugh put their finger on childhood woe and its embarrassments. But nightly dreams of deep blue water, of looking out from the crow's nest of a battered ship as it rounds a cliff, I owe to Le Guin. I can still close my eyes and count the sails. She owned me at age eight, on the overlit and understaffed second floor of a branch library in my DC neighborhood. Four decades and who knows how many rereadings later, she owns me still.[5]

The love I feel for these books comes partially from the happenstance of encountering them as a lonely and impressionable kid. Magic comes to you as a child promising to deliver you to a place that is not like the actual world. And then you discover leaving old rules behind does not mean a flight from all rules altogether. Forget the old rules; next minute you're busy learning new ones. Or inventing them yourself. The world she initially created I found myself bringing to life in my own way, inventing the stories that helped me put myself into the world alongside her characters.

That love also stems from my adult sympathy with Le Guin's anarchist aesthetics and her Taoism, both of which challenge any quick and easy comfort with the status quo. As a grown-up returning to that long-lost playground of the mind, I learned about the hold that invention can still have even when the first flush of enchantment is gone. Even our own world, material and unmagical all the way down, turns out to be imbued with beliefs that are not so easy to laugh away. Confirmed secularist that she was, Le Guin knew some things about what it means to believe.

Must Pictures Hold Us Captive?

Le Guin teaches her readers—both by constructing fantasy worlds and by deconstructing the reality within which we all live and breathe—that "secondary worlds" are not only found in the section of the library labeled fantasy. Although its creators may have been reluctant to admit its fantastical qualities, one of Le Guin's central ideas is that in some ways we've been living within a sort of collectively authored fantasy for as long as we've been human. The philosopher Ludwig Wittgenstein has a phrase for what happens when a fantasy passes itself off as simple reality: "a picture held us captive."[6] Not only did Le Guin learn how to conjure wizards, dragons, and the realm of the dead into being, she developed a sharp eye for the moments when similarly imaginative constructions were put forward as indisputable reality. In the second set of Earthsea books, Le Guin invites her readers to recognize the captivating pictures that hold us by depicting a world where just such sustaining illusions (captivating "pictures") fall away. Seeing imaginary chains unlocked in an imaginary land may be the best guide to unlocking the real ones in our actual world.

As she memorably put it in her 2014 National Book Award speech: "Capitalism['s] power seems inescapable. So did the divine right of kings."[7] Everything else she wrote could be taken as commentary on that single searing insight. Thinking may not *make* the world—but it does make sense of it. In some ways, that human capacity for invention is a very good thing. We share our world with a set of capacious consciousnesses endowed with imaginations that seize on different aspects of that world. Hannah Arendt celebrated the notion that each and every consciousness will experience that world anew, and she named that fundamental principle of existence *natality*.[8] Imagination is a beautiful and a shadowy builder.

However, invention can also lead us astray if we forget which parts of the stories unfolded around us daily are well-engineered masquerades. As anyone alive to the present-day operations of social media grasps intuitively, it can be hard to know when one is being presented with seeming truth that is actually a sly invitation to overlook important aspects of reality. Stories become true because people believe them: the divine right of kings, for instance. Then something happens to crack common sense—maybe a new fact in the world, maybe a new story—and a formerly captivating picture slips, letting reality peer in through the crack. Le Guin has a weather-eye for just such slips and cracks.

Ursula Kroeber, born in Berkeley to famous anthropologist parents—her mother Theodora wrote *Ishi in Two Worlds*—was eight days old on October 29, 1929. That does not make her a child of the Great Depression.[9] Like my own parents, she came of age in Eisenhower's America, when being white and middle class could seem to guarantee not only material but also metaphysical security.

Perhaps because her intellectual forcing-bed was that deceptively placid world, Le Guin loves to begin her books in places of seeming comfort. Sparrowhawk is tending goats on Gont in the first pages of *A Wizard of Earthsea*; *The Dispossessed* opens with Shevek the physicist on the moon Anarres, poor but free; in *The Lathe of Heaven* unremarkable George Orr is troubled by strange dreams in everyday Oregon. And then things start moving—which also means they start to go wrong in a way that suggests how wrong the reader was to think they were ever right. Sparrowhawk has magical powers—but his first real spell puts a rip in the world. Shevek's commune is no paradise—but leaving it is no cure. George's dreams change the world—but every good impulse ripples out into terrifying unintended consequences.

Le Guin needs her readers to believe in that easeful place, where feet are put up and eyes set on the horizon, so that all the *dis*-ease that follows has its proper contrast: to every shadow, its light.

Wherever you look in Le Guin there is solid ground—coupled with the sense that every path can twist and turn on you in an instant. This book is born out of my sense that the power in Le Guin stems from that doubleness—Earthsea is a foreign country that also feels like home. Because we find ourselves both in and out of sync with its imaginary valleys and seas, readers feel both that abiding ease children never forget and the glorious wrongness of magic, the sheer stomach-wrenching impossibility of a dragon glimpsed against the sun.

Fantasy as Parallax

Whether writing science fiction or fantasy, Le Guin is always moving away from her own world so as to see it better. Never was that more true than between 1968 and 1974. During the seven lean years her country suffered under Richard Nixon, Le Guin was not on the barricades; instead, she stood off to one side and told disturbing stories. The President offered mobilization, that familiar tactic of inventing unity by conjuring up a common enemy—later Republicans managed that trick even better. Against that false unity, Le Guin offered the sort of camaraderie that can only arise from respect for others' true autonomy. Her lonely dreamers, always on the move, only go astray when they imagine their solitary dreams might justify exercising authority over others.

Critics have often praised Le Guin for her commitment to solidarity. I can see why: she profoundly believes no one person is better than any other, and that we must all help one another or die trying. But her anarchist's vision of solidarity is predicated on *responsibility*. That is a word she repeated at least four times in the one and only conversation I had with her (a red-letter day in my life). She wants each person taking stock of what they themself know, and what it makes them decide. "Only following orders" isn't a remotely conceivable alibi in her worldview.

That is why it makes me happy to think of her sitting down to her typewriter every single day that Tricky Dick glowered in the White House. Her books remind us how little of our world belongs to those who think they rule it. Stalin said that the poet should be the engineer of human souls. Le Guin is the anti-engineer. Precise, evocative, and vivid as her writing is, we should think of it less as architecture than as road making: readers are not settled down by her writing, they are moved by it. Even her most polished books are open-ended and deliberately ragged. The final line of *The Left Hand of Darkness* is a boy's stammered question: "Will you tell us about other worlds out there among the stars—the other kinds of men, the other lives?"[10] Le Guin sets readers adrift among those worlds: peripatetic but somehow at home.

Other Roads to Le Guin

Earthsea is far from the only way into the Le Guin universe. She became a rarity by achieving a mainstream writerly reputation—Library of America volumes, National Book Award for Lifetime Achievement—without ever leaving speculative fiction behind. Other North Americans who straddle genres the same way form a select list: Philip K. Dick, Samuel Delany, Octavia Butler, Kurt Vonnegut, Margaret Atwood. Asking the question globally expands that list only slightly: Stanislaw Lem for sure, and more recently

Kazuo Ishiguro. Some might add Karel Capek, Borges, Italo Calvino, and Doris Lessing. Still, after adding your own two or three beloved authors, the category tops out around a baker's dozen.

Le Guin's poetry rates a mention, as do some beautiful translations, a version of the *Tao Te Ching*, and a lifetime of wide-ranging essays collected in books such as *The Language of the Night*. However, it is Le Guin's science fiction that forms an indispensable accompaniment to Earthsea. There are quirky but beautifully tuned stories throughout the 1960s before her "Hainish trilogy" of novels appeared in 1966 and 1967. Critical acclaim then arrived during the early Earthsea years—Hugos, Nebulas, and even a growing mainstream regard. After that, unchanged by the ebbing and flowing of her reputation, she piled up a long long career's worth of ambitious experiments, many now forgotten, others still prominently displayed in bookstores. My friend George, who studies eighteenth-century racial thinking, swears by *Five Ways to Forgiveness*, her fascinating suite of stories about slavery; my anthropologist pal Elizabeth loves *Always Coming Home*, an invented ethnography.

"The Ones Who Walk away from Omelas" (1973) is by far Le Guin's best known short story, but it has plenty of worthy company. I adore 1974's "The Day before the Revolution" and "The New Atlantis" (1975), a sly sideways look at a new island rising from the Pacific just as environmental catastrophe decimates Florida, California, and Le Guin's beloved Oregon. It is a witty sendup both of capitalist complacency and of the managerial socialism that Le Guin imagines coming after it—the heroine even has to hide her viola playing since classical music is not a sanctioned leisure activity.

Like much of her best work, "The New Atlantis" pivots away from acerbic satire in conclusion. The narrating heroine first makes a plan to leave the story's manuscript in a bottle given her by a friend—and then leaps forward to imagine the words of some aftercomers (Atlantisians? Aliens? Octopuses?) who will survey the wreckage of Oregon from their own distant time:

> When the brandy is gone I expect I will stuff this notebook into the bottle and put the cap on tight and leave it on a hillside somewhere between here and Salem. I like to think of it being lifted up little by little by the water, and rocking, and going out to the dark sea.[11]

Like so many of her later short stories "The New Atlantis" is at once a political commentary of the world as it is and a paean to the power of art as a force that can wrench the world sideways, simply by enabling people to see their own present in different terms. *See differently; act differently* might be her secret aesthetic credo.

Then there is the long-form science fiction that also came along during the first Earthsea years. Between 1968 and 1974 she published three other books that have rightly cemented her reputation. *The Lathe of Heaven* is a stunningly incisive reflection on the dark side of the notion of writer as a dreamy "world builder." It centers on George Orr, whose dreams can in fact alter reality. Her most sustained expostulation of anarchist politics in futuristic action comes in *The Dispossessed*—that story of the anarchists who escape to a moon colony to build their limited, stony, hard-fought new paradise is clearly responding to the socialist optimism of William Morris's *News from Nowhere*. And then there is the book depicted on the recently released Le Guin postage stamp. *The Left Hand of Darkness* even today reads as remarkably transgressive vision of gender; back in 1972 it was like a bolt from the blue.

It takes place on a planet where people live genderless almost all month, before pivoting, circumstances permitting, to three days of male or femaleness. Suddenly, the inescapability of categories like "men" and "women" fall away—just as the divine right of kings did, just as capitalism will in time.

It is Earthsea, though, that stays with me. Le Guin of all fantasy writers seems most aware of what it means to build a world up in the air, to furnish an apparatus around emptiness and make that emptiness itself into the art. Many great fantasy writers build vivid worlds—but they have wildly divergent ways of understanding what they do. C. S. Lewis thinks Narnia can be just as effective a twentieth-century Christian parable as Edmund Spencer's *The Faerie Queene* was in the sixteenth. Tolkien scorns Christian allegory, but counts his secondary world as a success only if readers forget its invented quality while reading it. Samuel Delany, poststructuralist and Nietzschean skeptic, never lets readers miss the irony of each self-referential page.

Le Guin is neither allegorist nor ironist. She delights in fantasy's striking mixture of tangible reality and airy nothingness. Le Guin's Earthsea books are animated in ways both explicit and implicit by the idea that "We have inhabited both the actual and the imaginary realms for a long time."[12] Central to every piece of fantasy and science fiction Le Guin wrote, that notion *of dual habitation* also forms the core of her politics, and her ethics.

Why Now?

Why this book, and why now? I passed two decades as an English professor happily teaching Victorian literature courses: Charles Dickens, Charlotte Brontë, Thomas Hardy, lots and lots of George

Eliot. That guaranteed me plenty of time discussing realism with students deeply immersed in Marxism, imperialism, and Orientalism. True, I wrote a children's book about William Morris that starred a talking bird, but that did not dim my enthusiasm for sitting down with students to anatomize power relations in settler-colonial societies.

About five years ago, however, I took an unexpected middle-age path back to Le Guin. Rilke looked at a statue of Apollo and heard a voice telling him: *"Du mußt dein Leben ändern"* (You must change your life).[13] Returning to Le Guin did something like that to me. There aren't many visible signs of that change: no sports cars, no family crisis, no running off to join the circus. Underneath, though, the tectonic plates shifted. This is a book about what Le Guin's imaginary places came to mean for me in our actual world.

That overwhelming sense you inhabit a world profoundly different from what you had believed: that is a Le Guin special. After you close her books, the magic never seems to dissipate fully. The Earthsea books are not what a recent taxonomy of fantasy calls "portal" fantasy: they do not feature characters from our own actual world making an explicit jump (via a painting or perhaps an enchanted wardrobe) into a fantasy world beyond.[14] Instead, they make the reader a dual inhabitant in a different way.

Le Guin novels turn on moments when characters suddenly discover the larger fabric into which their own thread is woven. Often, this begins with the simple discovery that others around one also have names, views, and quests all their own. That happens to Tenar early on in *The Tombs of Atuan*, when she is talking to her closest friend:

> There was something underneath Penthe's words with which she didn't agree, something wholly new to her, frightening to her. She

had not realized how very different people were, how differently they saw life. She felt as if she had looked up and suddenly seen a whole new planet hanging huge and populous right outside the window, an entirely strange world, one in which the gods did not matter.[15]

There's sly humor in a line like this, coming from a writer whose work it is to create just those new planets. Tenar had thought of herself as a world, as *the* world; now, all around her are other worlds, equally significant, looming equally large.[16]

Earthsea for Absolute Beginners

You may decide to go off and read (or reread) the Earthsea books before going any further. But if you are going to stay here instead, one thing you'll probably want is a quick description of the two Earthsea trilogies. Le Guin published the first trilogy—*A Wizard of Earthsea, The Tombs of Atuan, The Farthest Shore*—between 1968 and 1974. Taken together they remind me of that picture at the beginning of C. S. Lewis's *Voyage of the Dawn Treader*, the one that becomes a doorway into Narnia as the waves start moving and the pictured ship starts bobbing up and down. Like that painting, they aim to suck you straight in. My summary will never do Le Guin's lapidary and exquisitely straightforward storytelling justice. Still, here is a postage-stamp precis, with spoilers kept to a minimum.

A Wizard of Earthsea begins with Ged, a rash young goatherd from the provinces who foolishly summons up a dark force while training in the school for wizards on Roke Island. The quest that follows (half flight and half hunt) finds Ged parleying with dragons, drifting on a raft with mysterious sea-people beyond the edge of the known world before he confronts the *gebbeth* he unleashed. The spirit is evil, yes, but also a part of himself that has to be accepted rather than overcome. In *The Tombs of Atuan*, Ged is an older, careworn voyager, looking for the lost half of a totemic ring of peace. The central figure who controls his fate is Tenar, a young and virtually friendless priestess in a desert temple among the Kargish lands, in the eastern islands of Earthsea. Is the book Tenar's story, or Ged's? That's a question worth returning to, and puzzling over the way Le Guin herself did. *The Farthest Shore*, though, returns to Ged as Archmage of Roke, traveling with the young Arren in search of the dark mage Cobb who hopes to cheat death. Fighting that mad hubris takes Ged to the Land of the Dead—and costs him his magic powers just as Arren discovers his adult strength.

I was happy with my childhood Earthsea. Both for the enchantment it cast over me as a child and for what it made me feel all over again at fifty, looking back at its tiny clean blue-green gleam from the infinite expanses of adulthood—perhaps something like Milton's Satan first glimpsing Earth across the vastness of space.[17] And then, decades later, three more Earthsea books arrived. Le Guin came back to the world, revisited it, and informed her readers that things did not work quite the way they thought—not quite the way she had first imagined it. Without undoing the world, she opened up sightlines previously inconceivable. Some are variations within the world of magic: *What if dragons are not mankind's enemy but mankind itself?* Others, though, are more recognizable from the actual world: What if trauma could disrupt a life so thoroughly that no amount of storytelling could put it back on the same path?

By revisiting the world and regarding it from various other angles, the later books took that beautiful picture off the wall and put it into the middle of the room, with all sorts of aspects newly visible. Earthsea had turned from flat image into sculpture, a solid that required circumnavigation. As she noted in a late essay, "Earthsea Revisioned," Le Guin took a second pass at the dominant norms and mores of the earlier Earthsea cosmos. By doing so, she pushed readers into their own kind of revision. Le Guin's writing taught me that going forward sometimes involves turning back, even overturning. She thought a world into being for her readers; then by rethinking it invited all of us to think again as well.

Tehanu (1990) picks up with Tenar and Ged post-wizardry and adds a new protagonist, the fire-scarred and traumatized girl, Therru. Her terrible wounds are linked somehow to a metamorphosis that has come upon Earthsea itself. Either the girl and the world are both wounded—or their transfiguration foretells some new way of seeing how Earthsea is, and perhaps how it has always been. *Tales from Earthsea* (published in book form in 2001) is a medley of stories, delightful to read but hard to summarize. "Dragon Fly" is the clearest bridge to the changed new world of the final book, where seemingly fixed facts about gender and species start disintegrating in ways that reveal their original fictionality: "what everybody knows is true turns out to be what some people used to think."[18] Which might not be a bad mission statement for Le Guin's work as a whole: her fiction reminds readers that the pictures that held us captive in the past (from the divine right of kings to gender identities fixed at birth) are not categorically different from "what everybody knows is true" in the present moment.

The final Earthsea book, *The Other Wind* (also 2001) picks up with Ged and Tenar, and with Therru coming into her power as woman and dragon both. It also introduces Alder, a broken "mender" (of pots, mainly) who discovers in himself the power to break or mend the world entirely. Most of all, *The Other Wind* is about dragons and their strangeness and kindness to humans. It is a book about what makes for real difference, real kinship, and about the way that metamorphosis can reveal aspects of a world that have been present, unrecognized, all along,

I never would have written this book you are holding now without the second Earthsea trilogy. It is far less successful than the first trilogy—whether you measure success by sales, by critical reputation, or by impact on later fantasy writers, who voraciously pillaged the first trilogy for concepts like magical "true names," morally ambiguous dragons, and schools for wizards (yes, that idea too is original to Le Guin). I'd still stake a lot on the first Earthsea trilogy, plus *The Lathe of Heaven, The Dispossessed,* and *The Left Hand of Darkness.* But now I see that return to Earthsea over the subsequent decades as an act of great bravery, from a writer who never gave up exploring what it means to take action in the world, then return to that action and reconsider. If Henry James could follow his "major phase" with a "late phase" (including *The Golden Bowl* and *Wings of the Dove*) why couldn't Le Guin do the same?

To take a small example, those later Earthsea books poke underneath what had been a perfectly comfortable set of facts in the earlier books: that wizards never married, and had no sex life. In the first three books the male protagonist Ged is a wizard, born with power and then trained into its use at the Wizard's School on Roke. Wizards are celibate: while Ged is a wizard it does not even occur to him that he could have sexual (or for that matter romantic) feelings for someone else.

When the latter set of Earthsea books begins, it becomes apparent that what had felt like a power (wizardly celibacy) was also a problem. Moreover, what had seemed to be a natural law was only a manmade one—an invention masquerading as a fact of life. Now that Ged has lost his magic, suddenly the idea of sex—and along with it romantic love—becomes conceivable. A whole new set of plot possibilities emerges. Shaking off the clouds of their older mystification, the ex-sorcerer and the ex-priestess Tenar learn to see the world as it has always appeared to Moss, the neighborhood witch who never bothered to practice celibacy. Le Guin loves it when a set of perfectly sane-seeming normal assumptions about how to live and be and act in the world are revealed as far more arbitrary, far more local, and far more temporary than their practitioners imagine them to be.

This is what the best speculative fiction does: changes the scale of the universe that surrounds us and hence shifts the grounds of what counts as regular, as normal. Le Guin's fantasy is a special case, though. It creates both a solid, tangible material world—and that crazy sensation of falling, the realization that all you thought and knew was only what you thought you knew. That doubleness is what inspired me to write a final chapter exploring what happens to a Le Guin reader who returns as an adult. Le Guin went back, older and wiser, to make her world anew; the result was *Tehanu*, *Tales from Earthsea*, *The Other Wind*. I also returned to Earthsea, sporting new wrinkles if no new wisdom.

A Map

How should you navigate this book? Like a Le Guin character, you
have to decide what tack you will take. The first chapter, "Earthsea and the Fantasy Tradition," is a scholar's journey through the
century of speculative fiction that precedes Earthsea. Although
an unproductive faceoff between Christian and Marxist accounts
of fantasy has proven surprisingly dominant among scholars, I
take a different way in. That means exploring the implicit (and at
times explicit) debate between J. R. R. Tolkien's notion of fantasy
novels as self-contained "secondary worlds" and Samuel Delany's
opposing vision of fantasy as intimately and complexly linked to
our shared world. The tension between those two standpoints
brought me back to Le Guin, who offers a new way to think
about fantasy's distinctive role in our technology-filled world:
what the poet Yeats called "the cry of the heart against necessity."
My map-reader's advice, then: start with Chapter 1 if you want
to see speculative genres the way theorists and taxonomists of
literature do.

If Earthsea is the place for you, flip straight to Chapter 2, "Le
Guin's First Earthsea." There, I pack into one long chapter what
might make a book all its own: the notions of responsibility and
of naming, of balance and the virtues of inaction, of anarchism as
aesthetic practice that Le Guin spent a career exploring. Notions
she never expressed as beautifully and as lucidly as she did in
Earthsea. This is a chapter about the simple joy of reading Le
Guin. It also explores the complexity of the construction project
that goes into making that readerly pleasure so easily available.

Chapter 3, "Earthsea Revisited" looks at Le Guin's own rereading—and rewriting—of her world after a decades-long hiatus. This second trilogy is not so much an undoing or an apology as it a new circumnavigation. Suddenly, unexpected second and third angles alter the look of everything you thought you knew from that first view. Trauma rears its head, and history too—and fluidity replaces the seeming solidity of certain fixed differences: between genders, between species, between the living and the dead.

Finally, Chapter 4, "My Earthsea" is an occasion to talk about why fantasy and science fiction still remain so central to my own imaginative and professional life. It begins, though, from an appreciation of all the things that Le Guin does to make her books available to her readers—in fact how she *empties out* Earthsea, in the best possible way. Le Guin is always devoted to creating a space those who come after can inhabit as their own.

In 1997 Le Guin produced an "English version" of Laozi's *Tao Te Ching*, a labor of love that took her many years to complete. It is fascinating in its own right, and also for the guidance it gives to the sources of Le Guin's own philosophy of action, and of aesthetic creation. For me, reading Poem 11 of Book One "The Uses of Not," opened a lane to Le Guin's ethos:

> Hollowed out,
> Clay makes a pot.
> Where the pot's not
> Is where it's useful.
> Cut doors and windows
> To make a room.
> Where the room isn't
> There's room for you.[19]

This conception of aesthetic creation is sly, funny, and a million miles deep. Art like Le Guin's is at its best creating a space for its audience. The reality of artwork lies not in the material—the clay, the glass, the words on the page—but in the opening it makes.

Willa Cather's remarkable manifesto, "The Novel Démeublé," proposes that fiction ought to be an empty room, stripped of furniture so that the reader can walk in and hear the emptiness:

> It is the inexplicable presence of the thing not named, of the overtone divined by the ear but not heard by it, the verbal mood, the emotional aura of the fact or the thing or the deed, that gives high quality to the novel or the drama, as well as to poetry itself … How wonderful it would be if we could throw all the furniture out of the window; and along with it, all the meaningless reiterations concerning physical sensations, all the tiresome old patterns, and leave the room as bare as the stage of a Greek theatre, or as that house into which the glory of Pentecost descended.[20]

Like Cather, Le Guin is not so much obedient to her readers as *mindful* of them, of the space within which they can get to work imagining. She has hollowed out this pot, emptied this room, for readers' benefit: the "room for you" within her work is a way to find your own level.

That empty space is not simply the aftereffect of the artwork; it actually *is* the artwork. Think of this as the story of Le Guin's pot, then, as told by one potful of water: an inside story.

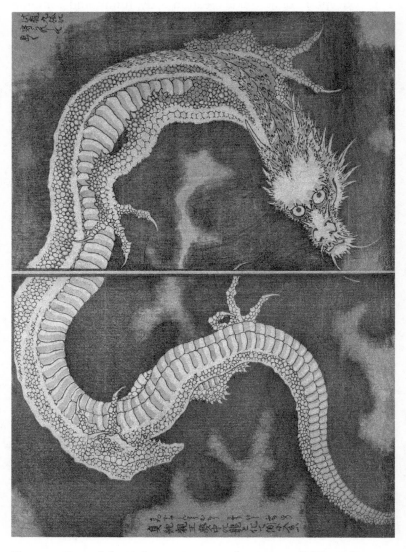

Figure 2 Katsushika Hokusai's *Picture Book on Heroes of China and Japan* (1850), Metropolitan Museum Collection Open Access Program. Purchase, Mary and James G. Wallach Foundation Gift, 2013.

CHAPTER I

EARTHSEA AND THE FANTASY TRADITION

My "Fantasy Worlds" class at Brandeis is generally chrono-logical. We debate whether the epic of Gilgamesh counts as fantasy in week two, take on Lucian's *True Story* (140 AD) and its moon spiders in week three, trundling onward toward a final class on N. K. Jemisin's 2015 *The Fifth Season*. However, the first week is dedicated to *A Wizard of Earthsea*. That's an anachronism but not an absurdity: Le Guin is an exemplary fantasy novelist as well as an exceptional one. That book's exploration of the difference between actuality and the imaginative realm just over the horizon gives my students everything they need to get going: a young wizard, spells gone wrong, an education that is not quite the right preparation to battle evil. And always dragons riding the wind on the horizon.

The secret of Le Guin, perhaps the secret of fantasy altogether, lies in those dragons. When she asks "Why Are American Afraid of Dragons?" her answer is that modern readers—and she clearly has a wider readership than just US residents in mind—live in a world fixated on economic success mainly attainable by way of technological proficiency: "I suspect that almost all very highly technological peoples are more or less antifantasy." That means we confine our most extravagant flights of fantasy "to the ultimate escapist reading ... that masterpiece of total unreality, the daily stock market report." By ignoring the fantastical nature of the whole monetary system that underpins our existence, we have cut ourselves off from the sort of fantasy that features dragons instead of stock-tickers.

On the one hand, by Le Guin's telling, there are the made-up stories we have tricked ourselves into thinking they are facts (like the "value" of stocks); on the other hand there is the unreal truth that resides in invented dragons. To grow up in America as Le Guin sees it, is to forego the truth in dragons for the deceitful facticity of the stock market. Adults, sadly, "are afraid of dragons, because they are afraid of freedom."[1] If choosing dragons over stock-prices makes sense to you, Le Guin has done her work well. It may be hard to reconstruct just how bold it was to make that kind of that claim for fantasy when Le Guin stepped onto the scene in the 1960s. In 2023, turning on the television to see queens in command of CGI dragons is almost routine. As banal as taking in the latest Tolkien movie, or seeing bookstore shelves stacked with fantastical or speculative novels by canonized blue-chip novelists: the list starts but doesn't end with David Mitchell, Kazuo Ishiguro, Gary Shteyngart, Karl Ove Knausgard, Jennifer Egan.

Le Guin wrote in a different time. Fantasy addicts like me can certainly point beyond the experimental fiction of J. L. Borges and Italo Calvino and the magical realism of Gabriel Garcia Marquez to a few 1960s outliers. No true fantasy lover should overlook early work by Argentine fantasist Angelica Gorodischer (Le Guin translated her 1983 *Kalpa Imperial*) and the remarkable "kingdoms of Elfin" *New Yorker* stories by Sylvia Townsend Warner. Still, compared to the present moment, or to the glory days of George MacDonald and William Morris a century earlier (not to mention the heyday of Arthurian legends many centuries before that) fantasy was at a distinctly low ebb in 1969, the year Ballantine began the Adult Fantasy series that Jamie Williamson credits with fashioning the genre, or at least refashioning it for the present.[2] And it was lower still two years earlier, when Le Guin, just coming off a very successful series of science fiction novels (*Rocannon's World, Planet of Exile,* and *City of Illusions*) accepted what may have been the earliest commission for a "young adult" book.

The Fantastical Path to Le Guin

If someone were to ask you what writers changed how you see the world and act within it, whom would you pick? Hannah Arendt was such a writer for me; Willa Cather too. Yet when I got the call to write about *My Reading,* I knew it had to be Le Guin. The chapters that follow spell out a dozen reasons for that feeling. Before anything else, though, there's Le Guin's crucial role in the modern rejuvenation of prose fantasy. And that role has everything to do with her connection to the centuries of writing that preceded her.

Here is a contrast that may help clarify Le Guin's importance in ensuring fantasy's continued relevance as a speculative genre in our technologized and very un-magical world. I admire the political passion of Kim Stanley Robinson, whose recent "cli-fi" trilogy imagines catastrophic climate change starting to drown Manhattan sometime in the coming century. But Robinson's idea about the role speculative fiction can play nowadays is that "Science Fiction is the great realism of our time." To him, science fiction works primarily by showing us a realistic snapshot of our future: *extrapolation* is his keyword.[3]

Le Guin, however, thinks that centering speculative fiction (science fiction and fantasy both) on extrapolation is a mistake, an impoverished description of what non-realist prose can do. She says so outright in the 1976 Introduction for *The Left Hand of Darkness*: "Though extrapolation is an element of science fiction, it isn't the name of the game by any means … [Instead] read [this book] … as a thought-experiment."[4] Le Guin's resistance to the logic of extrapolation applies in spades to her fantasy. Le Guin readers are never meant to ask: *could my own world end up that way, eventually?* Instead, her fantasy poses the questions that Menippean satire asks: *why should we conceive things in this way?* And: *what happens if we start conceiving them in another way altogether?*

Fantastic worlds are clearly not an extrapolation from the present. Magic is one word for the sort of otherness fantasy introduced. But perhaps another way to think about the essence of fantasy is to recall that its authors are creating a world that isn't, that couldn't possibly be our own. Le Guin finds one memorable way to frame that contrast: we have stock markets; they have dragons. That contrast explains a curiously underdiscussed aspect of the genre's history: that adult prose fantasy gained its greatest successes just a few decades into the Industrial Revolution, when technology was vanquishing magic everywhere you looked. Ironically, nineteenth-century fantasy novelists succeeded by ignoring the robust scientific materialism of the Industrial Age. Fantasy novelists turned their eyes from their own era deliberately: there is no steam-punk in the nineteenth century. George MacDonald's 1858 *Phantastes*, for example, is frequently considered the first example of modern prose fantasy for adults: its schizoid, slightly Dadaesque and dreamlike style links it closely both to William Morris's late wonderful prose romances (e.g., *The Sundering Flood*) and to later risqué works like James Branch Cabell's *Jurgen*.[5] Like Lewis Carroll's *Alice in Wonderland*, it decisively departs from the irksome demands of the humdrum "real world."

Fantasy's impulse to escape has as much to tell us about the way reality appeared to residents of the fin de siècle industrial era as do the grim determinism of naturalist novels about Chicago's stockyards or Parisian markets. Yet scholars have been reluctant to include the emergent genre of adult prose fantasy in charting the late-nineteenth- and early-twentieth-century impact of scientific empiricism and technological modernity. Why? That is a long story, but part of the answer is that two scholarly tendencies have influentially undervalued fantasy's relationship to the more realist or quasi-realist genres that apparently dominated the realm of fiction in the Victorian and the modernist era. One of those critical traditions is a largely historical Christian apologism with ties to Northrop Frye's work on generic archetypes; the other, surprisingly, is Marxist historicism. For very different reasons, each tradition systematically overlooked the most interesting connections between fantasy and mainstream fiction of those eras. The former tendency is incarnate in Colin Manlove, Northrop Frye acolyte and seeker for Christian patterns; the latter helps explain Frederic Jameson.

Manlove, in *The Impulse of Fantasy Literature*, decries the "unreflecting stupor" and "anemic" fantasizing writers who fail to suture their stories onto a recognizable (implicitly or explicitly Christian) quest-motif.[6] Manlove is repulsed by the material impulse in fantasy—e.g., in Oscar Wilde and William Morris, both of whom he accuses of mere decadent posturing that blocks the proper fantastical turn toward suitably teleological Christian motifs. In *Archaeologies of the Future*, by contrast, Jameson

proposes a binary between science fiction understood as historically emancipatory (because realist in its investment in Hegelian
progress), and the static errors of "Fantasy—that is to say daydreaming in the Freudian sense."[7] In doing so, he follows squarely
in the path laid out by science-fiction-criticism godfather Darko
Suvin, whose formative article on science fiction's "cognitive
estrangement" via "the novum" explicitly contrasts science fiction
to fantasy's rigidity and conservative devotion to static mythic
givens. Suvin juxtaposes science fiction's innovations to fantasy, which is "committed to the interposition of anti-cognitive
laws into the empirical environment."[8] Jameson and Suvin deem
fantasy distasteful in its mere idealism.[9]

If Jameson needs to demonize fantasy in order to praise the scientific Marxism of admirable science fiction, Manlove aims to dis-
tinguish within fantasy between the spiritually teleological (Christian) and what he dubs the decadent or formless investigation of
value. Looking back at the modern fantasy's history through the
lens of Le Guin, however, enables us to admire it for its power of
non-technological invention, and for its delight in forms of non-
religious belief. Looking back via Le Guin also helps us to see fantasy at work everywhere, even where we have been trained to see
nothing but realism.

Taken for a Goddess: Realism's Fantasy

Fantasy is a disreputable genre that easily gets labeled either as
"popular" or "juvenile" as a way of avoiding close encounters with
individual works. Saying a book is written for or read by children
does not always prevent scholars taking it seriously: look at *Alice*

in Wonderland. However, once a text is designated "genre fiction" its best hope is to stand in as a representative sample, rather than a unique artwork. So if one wants to make a case for the surprising importance of fantasy in a secular modern age, there is little profit in starting with avowed fantasy writers like Lord Dunsany or Stella Benson, much as I love them.[10] It is just too easy to ignore writers already carefully tucked away into obscure pigeonholes.

E. M. Forster has impeccable realist bona fides: *A Room with a View, Passage to India, Howards End*. Yet he also has underappreciated roots in fantasy. From his earliest short fiction to his late madcap speculative fragments, he wrote frequently about an odd kind of fairy-space where the Ideal can come into conversation and into open conflict with the merely material aspects of actual existence; for example, a very fantastical "greensward" emerges as a redemptive oasis at the end of his late realist novel *Maurice*. The way in which key ideas and tropes of fantasy pervade his realist fiction sheds a surprising light on fantasy's relationship to its neighboring genres. Even in Forster works that seem nothing more than ordinary realist fiction we can see the glinting shards of fantasy shining through. Forster's realism is so poignant because he first shows his characters imagining the glories of the world as it could be— if, for example, forbidden sexual desires could speak their name, something Forster knew a great deal about. Then he slams those characters back into the world as it actually is.

W. B. Yeats once called his own early work "the cry of the heart against necessity."[11] By *necessity* Yeats means the complete material basis of the world we live in—and he also means the belief that everything in such a universe is determined, fixed into place by knowable laws. His heart is not the first one to cry out against that—and to seek recourse from it in fantasy. Some seek a more durable solace in religion, where belief is elevated into an unapologetic force more powerful than knowledge, institutionally enshrined with devotional books to read and social events (weekly services for example) that point to the sure and certain hope of an answer from beyond the empirical realm. Forster, though is part of the same fantasy tradition that Yeats belongs to—one in which religion's safeguards are less substantial than they claim to be. Instead, he accepts that knowledge of our shared empirical actuality can't be superseded or replaced by belief—without giving up on the obscure desire (the *heart's cry*) for things to be otherwise,

When Le Guin named the writers of the modernist era who shaped her, she singled out more overtly fantastical texts—Kipling's *Jungle Book*, Lord Dunsany, Tolkien. Nonetheless, writers like Forster pave the most interesting way toward the fantasy revival that Le Guin spearheaded a half-century later. To understand why, we need to appreciate the ghostly presence of a non-material realm in all of Forster's fiction—and especially in his 1905 *Where Angels Fear to Tread*.

As Forster himself announced, it is in his early stories—among them "The Other Side of the Hedge," "The Other Kingdom," and "The Celestial Omnibus"—that "Fantasy … can be caught in the open … by those who care to catch her."[12] Those other worlds he had been conjuring up had prepared him well to write realist fiction that charted just how crucial the power of the fantastical, the imaginative, and the non-actual remains—even in a fully material universe. *Where Angels Fear to Tread* shows readers that even in a world now scientifically known to be without fairies and angels, the heart's cry that produces a lingering belief in fairies and angels still matters.

The novel's plot is straightforward: a young English widow, Lillia Herriton, travels to Italy and falls in love with an unsuitably déclassé dentist's son, Gino. After her death, her brother-in-law Philip and a friend, Caroline Abbott, set out to recover Lillia's baby. At the novel's heart are the incompatible ways Caroline and Philip (the would-be baby rescuers) come to fall in love with an Italy that is also a fantasy world for them, a place where dreams come to life. Both find themselves, as anyone entering fairyland will, in "the presence of something greater than right or wrong."

Faced with an Italy that seems both marvelous and tangible, Philip preaches the virtues of detached daydreaming. You can escape from English narrowness, he tells Caroline, because you have the mental freedom simply to daydream:

> Society is invincible—to a certain degree. But your real life is your own and nothing can touch it. There is no power on earth that can prevent your criticizing and despising mediocrity—nothing that can stop you retreating into splendor and beauty—into the thoughts and beliefs that make the real life—the real you.[13]

Because he has been seeking this kind of dreamy internal exile, Philip tells Caroline ruefully late in the novel, he perennially finds himself "fated to pass through the world without colliding with it or moving it."[14] Like a subatomic particle or a ghost, he finds himself an insubstantial shade in the world he longs to enter.

Caroline's response to Italy makes an admirable counterpoint to Philip's. She also finds herself frequently overwhelmed by her experience of the country—most memorably when she goes to reclaim Lillia's baby from his father, Gino, and finds him standing, faunlike, with his foot on the stomach of his baby in all the pride of possession. Looking at Gino's relationship with his son, Caroline (unlike Philip) finds a world worth entering, to possess and be possessed by. As she sees it, Gino is

> filled with the desire that his son should be like him and should have sons like him, to people the earth. It is the strongest desire that can come to a man—if it comes to him at all—stronger even than love or the desire for personal immortality.[15]

Philip is the angel who "fears to tread": he finds it better to dream apart from the world and not meddle with its actuality. Caroline, seemingly, is the fool who rushes in, loving Gino not despite but because of his pure carnal delight in the world as is, loving his bare foot on his baby's skin.

Reviewers at the time generally saw Forster taking Philip's side, praising the virtues of aesthetic detachment and reserve. However, it is the substantial and openly desiring Caroline rather than the ethereal Philip whose fate matters most at the novel's conclusion. The novel's true tragedy is not that Philip fails to woo Caroline: that possibility, introduced suddenly at the novel's end, is tenuous and emotionally unpersuasive. Its actual climax comes when Caroline fails to win Gino.

Ironically, it is not his earthiness that foils them. Rather, Gino turns out to have the same flaw as Philip. When it comes to making sense of Caroline's love for him, his angelic preconceptions about her nature hold him back. Caroline tells Philip ruefully that Gino did not see in Caroline what she saw in him: "all through he took me for a superior being—a goddess."[16] In other words, the most terrifying thing about fantasy is the way that we allow it to shape our sense of the world we live in. The heart does not cry out against necessity only in high-flung poetry: it does so every day, as we make up fantastical stories about those around us.[17] To

Caroline, Gino is quite a man. To Gino, unfortunately, Caroline is more than human. She doesn't seem to him to exist on his own plane of being. They pass one another, or even pass through one another, ghosts or subatomic particles, somehow inhabiting the same space without real interaction.

Rather than a set of stories in books mainly for children, fantasy comes across in Forster as a disposition in the shared actual world, an omnipresent tendency we have to fantasize about one another. If antique forms of fantasy begin with a goddess being mistaken for a woman, Forster's novel tells the sad story of a woman unable to find love because she is mistaken for a goddess. Forster suggests that although fantastic forces like angels may not actually exist in the world, we retain our belief in them—and that belief proves to be a powerful force within our disenchanted world. Inside Forster's realist fiction, such fantastical conceptions (woman taken for goddess) reveal how thoroughly everyone's ordinary experience of the world is grounded as much on unproveable beliefs as on definite knowledge of the surrounding world. Even in a world without actual gods and goddesses, fantasy fuels and shapes reality.

Fantasy, not Science Fiction

> Only in silence the word,
> only in dark the light,
> only in dying life:
> bright the hawk's flight on the empty sky.
> —*The Creation of Éa*[18]

That surprising link between fantasy and realism makes it easier to turn back to the question of what makes fantasy different from the science fiction that Robinson praises as the "realism of our time." Darko Suvin argues that science fiction is defined by the presence of a technical innovation (he calls it a *novum*) that produces "cognitive estrangement" in readers. That is, science fiction's story space is linked to the actual world in rational ways, by history and scientific possibility (hence *cognitive*): yet (*estrangement*) the world depicted is unsettlingly different, because of a transformative *novum*: a time machine, a faster-than-light drive, a sentient computer.[19] As Suvin and Jameson see it, fantasy by contrast generates an escapist world that signals its complete disconnection from our own everyday reality. Suvin censoriously calls this recourse to magic "anti-cognitive."[20]

I think, though, that fantasy's turn to magic should be explained, rather than explained away. Far better to embrace the genre's distinctiveness than disavow it. Its greatness lies not in extrapolation but in sheer speculation, predicated on the human capacity to invent, and invent anew, and to invent on top of invention. A passing remark in Flann O'Brien's fantastical *The Third Policeman* captures this aspect of fantasy's world-building well: "Anything can be said in this place and it will be true and will have to be believed."[21] There is an ungenerous reading of such "yes ... and" logic. You can choose to think of this invention as avoiding the "real" rules of the game. When Suvin and Jameson speak of fantasy as daydreaming, they mean that it refuses to play by rules they think of as indispensable. Just as free verse is "tennis without a net," fantasy strikes Suvin as estranging without being rationally "cognitive."

I see the separation between science fiction and fantasy differently. Magic is not a cop-out, it is a chance to invent the world anew and play a new set of games according to different rules–anyone who has played tag or basketball on a temporarily repurposed tennis court knows the feeling. Fantasy worlds are more than simply an extension of random writerly dreams; they also entail their own answerability to its logic and its expanding lore. The author has to take responsibility for what the world contains (there is a resonant Yeats title: "In Dreams Begin Responsibilities").

That can be daunting for the reader, who might prefer a set of world-rules mastered a long time ago. Yet consider the immense imaginative undertaking they represent: they are like creating a new bacterium out of strands of DNA, or even out of atoms painstakingly strung together. Long before Le Guin, that power of radical invention was fantasy's stock-in-trade. It shows up in writers from centuries past: long before William Morris and Tolkien, there is a line that stretches back to such medieval romance writers like Marie de France and a millennium earlier, the comic genius Lucian of Samosata. And it has flourished since (thanks in part to Le Guin): Samuel Delany, N. K. Jemisin, and Marlon James are evidence of ongoing vitality.

In fact, one key proof of the dynamic potential of the genre's power of invention is the sheer variety of kinds of connection between our actual world and invented fantasy worlds.[22] Samuel Delany's *Neveryon* series, for example, came along in the decades after Earthsea's first trilogy. I love the way it tells the story of capitalism's rise and spread by way of the mysterious appearance, in a rough-and-tumble medieval world, of the first modern trade-good: little bouncing rubber balls that Neveryonians covet and trade in an almost fetishistic way. And I love that in 1984 Delany wrote "The Tale of Plagues and Carnivals"—arguably the first piece of long fiction about AIDS. Although the piece mentions AIDS and Greenwich Village by name, the deadly outbreak that it focuses on is set inside the quasi-medieval and magical world of Neveryon. Delany is unsurpassed in using made-up worlds to extrapolate and explore the perturbing currents of desire that invented differences can start moving within a society: there is, for example, a lot of (very unLeGuinian) sexual "cosplay" involving people who willingly don or pretend to don slave collars. There are even dragons in Delany's world—pampered but still malevolent reptilian gliders, who have problems getting airborne.

But those dragons, like his collar-wearing slaves and pampered lordlings, exist within a world of political negotiations that he represents as ultimately fueled by the same emotional currents he also charts when writing about West Village life in the 1980s. Delany does not forego fantasy's inventiveness; instead he turns it back into the service of an analysis of our own world.[23] The way Delany manages that suggestive overlay between Neveryon and Manhattan is completely unlike the way that Le Guin crafts an Earthsea that exists apart from our own world in every regard. Yet his writing is in the spirit of Le Guin's refusal to apologize for choosing invention over extrapolation.

There is much more to be said about Le Guin's fantasy style and her sense of that style. In the next chapter I dig into the distinctive features that make Le Guin's fantasy world so tangible, and that make her writing so endlessly thought-provoking: the magical power of true names, her style, her preference for story over plot, her notion of responsibility in place of mobilization, and her skepticism about the virtues of action. This chapter about the genealogy of the fantasy genre Le Guin inherited should end, though, with her conception of her writing's place within the larger world of fiction. She insists repeatedly and in various ways that her kind of fantasy is not *tainted* by being completely made up. Being made-up is the point—that is what makes fantasy great. In the best fantasy worlds, she maintains, "There is only a construct built in a void, with every joint and seam and nail exposed."[24]

As Le Guin understands the power of fantasy, escape is not escapism. In *The Lathe of Heaven*, George Orr, the dreamer whose dreams come true, plays the role of a fantasy writer who looks up to find his fantasy has been written into actuality. George dreams up a war, an alien invasion, a plague that kills off 95 percent of humanity.[25] Yet Le Guin does not apologize for this kind of world-remaking. Instead she contemplates it as a basic human power, an impulse that sometimes should be restrained, other times acknowledged. Earthsea is made up, the world George Orr dreams is made up ("not even probable!" he exclaims at one point). But so too is our own home country, so too is our own life on Earth in 2022. Le Guin's fiction's great virtue is that it trains a spotlight on all the things that we do make up, and then treat as if they were real as rocks. Le Guin is out to remind her readers of what that kind of rewriting (re-dreaming the world, you might say) has in common with the everyday affirming of reality we all perform simply by believing in shared beliefs that make up the truths to which our culture and country pledges daily implicit allegiance.

In fantasy's audacity about that act of invention lies its strength. Most things we hear and see in a given day are present as if they were unmediated, as if their underlying truth could be taken for granted. But readers of Le Guin open the book knowing that what confronts them is invention through and through. So readers look over those joints and seams and nails and decide if this delightfully made-up world holds. If it does, then together writer and reader have forged the very thing Tenar discovered in *The Tombs of Atuan*, when she suddenly found herself looking at things through Penthe's eyes: a new planet hanging up there.

Figure 3 Leonardo Da Vinci's "A Design for a Dragon Costume" (c.1517–18) from the Royal Collection (RCIN 912369).

CHAPTER 2

LE GUIN'S FIRST EARTHSEA

There is a tale told in the East Reach of a boat that ran aground, days out from any shore, over the abyss of ocean ... So of the song of the Shadow there remain only a few scraps of legend, carried like driftwood from isle to isle over the long years.[1]

If you think you have Le Guin pegged because you know young adult fantasy, think again. Like other protean, inventive fantasists, Le Guin drops her reader into an uncanny double of our own world, a dream where somebody changed the names and shapes of everything.[2] This chapter aims to account for how she works her magic by approaching Earthsea from many directions. Like different routes up the same mountain, each unveils distinct features concealed from another vantage.

There are many ways to account for Le Guin's Earthsea durable afterlife in its readers' minds, and an array of accomplished scholars and writers have taken on that task.[3] At times, I have felt that Le Guin's peculiar gift is to make the ordinary feel as important as the epic. Mundane questions about who's cutting firewood or doing the dishes share space with rune books and miscast spells. Viewed in that way, her Earthsea has less in common with Narnia and Percy Jackson's Camp Half-Blood than it does with medieval romances and Icelandic sagas, where dragons and death keep company with fishing yarns, shepherding woes, and village quarrels.

Then there are moments when Le Guin's genius seems to lie in her characters: the young wizard who is first Sparrowhawk then Ged, Tenar the child/priestess/goddess incarnate, Arren who learns what it is to rule by learning to accept what is outside his control. Sometimes, by contrast, understanding Le Guin involves noticing how adventures and seemingly trivial episodes pile up to become not the novel's plot but its *story* (crucial Le Guin distinction). And there are those marvelous quests and journeys, central to Le Guin's restless, peripatetic way of knowing-by-visiting, which she inherits from William Morris, Tolkien, and a long line of medieval predecessors. That question of influence turns out to be a tricky area, though, because it lays bare Le Guin's quarrel with herself ("We make out of the quarrel with others, rhetoric, but of the quarrel with ourselves, poetry")[4] as regards her own youthful debt to the racist and sexist legacy of European folklore.[5]

I have also seen her writing through the eyes of her great admirer Kim Stanley Robinson, who praised her "ability to compress and to find the beautiful phrase ... to go with the power of poetry alone." Robinson went on to say Le Guin did not "need or want ... the intensive realist details that might make something feel more substantial."[6] It may be a small distinction, but I would praise her style in slightly different terms: Le Guin generates a world that is vividly present to her readers precisely *because* of the poetic compression, the lyric intensity of her description.

So many ways in: Where to begin? Starting this chapter with Le Guin's style might make it seem that the basic building-block of Le Guin's magic was the sentence. Every dragon-fearing and magic-loving reader will tell you that Earthsea's truest building-block is something much smaller: the true name.

Names and the Old Speech

> There is a language in which all things bear their true names, and deed and word are one. By speaking that tongue Segoy raised the islands from the deeps. It is the language dragons speak.[7]

Many things change between the first Earthsea trilogy and the sequels decades later. Ogion's dying words in *Tehanu* (book 1 of the second trilogy) set the tone: "Over … All changed!" The line between dragons and humans comes down, the seemingly immutable enmity between Kargish and Hardic lands dissolves, even the wall between the living and the dead is disassembled.

One thing does not change. The bedrock of magic in Earthsea is the power associated with the speech of creation, in which all things and all people bear their true names. From start to finish dragons speak the Old Tongue, humans cannot speak it falsely, and all spells are cast in it. Only when called by its true name will a rock (*tolk*) change its shape; only when their true name is spoken can human beings be enchanted, or immobilized, or worse. In order for Sparrowhawk finally to tame the dark spirit (*gebbeth*) that he has summoned with ill-advised magic, he has to realize that its true name is the same as his: Ged.

Small wonder that one of the two fledgling Earthsea stories from back in 1964, three years before Le Guin decided to set novels there, was called "The Rule of Names." Like many episodes in the Earthsea novels themselves, that story turns on the power-granting discovery of someone's name. In Earthsea, the true names of the objects and persons are hard to master, restricted to wizards to learn. In fact, the difference between men and women with magic powers may come down to this: that men have the opportunity to go to Roke to learn those names and how to use them, so becoming mages or wizards. Witches, meanwhile, are never trained because never respected—or never respected because never trained. Chicken, meet egg.

Every crucial episode in the Earthsea books turns at least in part on just how much a wizard can do with the right proper name. With a dragon's name for instance. Early on in *A Wizard*, when Ged speaks with a dragon for the first time in his life, he quickly reveals that his last best weapon in this David–Goliath fight is … archival research. *How will a puny thing like you thwart me?* asks the colossal dragon as they do battle out in the lonely islet-studded western Reaches. It is a rhetorical question and a mocking one at that, but Ged has an answer:

> "With your name, Yevaud."
> Ged's voice shook as he spoke the name, yet he spoke it clear and loud. At the sound of it, the old dragon held still, utterly still. A minute went by, and another; and then Ged standing there in his rocking chip of a boat, smiled. He had staked this venture and his life on a guess drawn from old histories of dragon-lore learned on Roke, a guess that this Dragon of Pendor was the same that had spoiled the west of Osskil in the days of Elfarran and Morred, and had been driven from Osskill by a wizard, Elt, wise in names. The guess had held.[8]

A known name stops time, confers power.

How should we understand this power of names, and its durability throughout the Earthsea series? Names make the world come alive, make it responsive to the touch. To tame the sea for instance a wizard cannot use the general word for sea but has to know the true name of the particular patch of sea, the bay or estuary or channel or open space that he wishes to calm. Specificity is all—and the power of names is that they delineate a proper-sized bundle: be that an acre of sea or a particular human being.

One simple point about the power of names and words spoken in the dragon tongue is that Le Guin's framing the magic this way heightens the parallel between novelist and magician. Wizards and writers share the power to call something into the world using only words.[9] When George Orr's dreams alter the world in *The Lathe of Heaven*, Le Guin unapologetically literalizes the novelist's identity as a dreamer who calls reality into being. That's one axis on which the analogy between writer and character can run: both are dreamers, both have the power, the horrifying and unsought power, to bring change to the seeming permanence of the world by thinking it otherwise. But the power that wizards in Earthsea possess is far more subtle, and far more litigated within the series. You might think of them as users of language who are sometimes able, with much practice and much restraint, to make the right words in the right order alter the world. Wittgenstein has an evocative epigram for this case: "To imagine a language means to imagine a form of life."[10]

Spellwords

So far I have been referring to the power of "names" in Earthsea, but there is another word to describe these elements of the Old Speech: "spellwords." That more capacious term focuses less on the name itself than the linguistic system within which magic is suspended. That will set some readers wondering about the dark side of such power: does magic corrupt by nature, simply by virtues of the controlling force it can exert? Le Guin certainly entertains that proposition.

Late in the final book Alder—a magician who has lost his power—asks a simple but startling question: if mankind cannot lie in the Old Speech, what need was there of another kind of speech? His teacher Gannet had told him to be cautious using the words he knew, because

> "Spellwords act ... Each is a deed of power ... True word makes truth be."
> ... [wizards] preferred not to use them in conversation, but to keep to ordinary language which, if it allowed lies and errors, also permitted uncertainty and retraction. Perhaps that had been part of the great choice men made in ancient times: to give up the innate knowledge of the Old Speech, which they once shared with the dragons. Had they [adopted new languages], Alder wondered, in order to have a language of their own, a language suited to mankind, in which they could lie, cheat, swindle, and invent wonders that never had been and would never be?[11]

This dark way of thinking about language as lying would be right at home in the Samuel Delany fantasy series I praised earlier, *Nevèrÿon*. There Delany treats power, violence, and authority as three interwoven, perhaps indistinguishable concepts.

When Delany lays out ways in which the marking down of names in Nevèrÿon leads quickly to enslavement, the parallels to our own world are self-evident:

> If you can write down a woman's or man's name, you can write down all sorts of things next to that name, about the amount of work they do, the time it takes for them to do it, about their methods, their attitudes, and you can compare all this very carefully with what you have written about others. If you do this, you can maneuver your own dealings with them in ways that will soon control them; and very soon you will have the control over your fellows that is slavery.[12]

As Delany puts it here, writing is innately untrustworthy because its instrumentality is its most salient feature: it was created to enslave.

Even when she writes about those who use magic to warp others to their will, however, Le Guin quickly moves to reject the notion that such power exists in a *purely* malignant and instrumental form. At one point in the Afterword to *Tales from Earthsea*, Le Guin describes her story "On the High Marsh" as letting her "deal with what gets left out when magic is understood purely as power."[13] Le Guin means to refute this way of thinking: in Earthsea magic is not understood as principally a tool of domination, even though it may be used to dominate. The magic of spellwords in Le Guin remains aligned with the magic of a language in which humans can invent extravagant stories like *The Deed of Ged*. Language does magic simply by being linguistic.

Rereading Le Guin's late "Description of Earthsea" recently, I was struck by how carefully she tiptoes around the question of *precisely* what sort of magic resides in language. I think she means it to be something of a koan, a philosophical puzzle. For example, dragons do not learn but are born knowing the Old Speech, since their ancestors long ago chose not to live on Earth like humans, but to embrace the propertyless freedom and endless movement of the air. Hence the final Earthsea book's title, *The Other Wind*. Because dragons live in and in some sense *are* that wind, that ceaseless breath of the planet, "the dragon and the speech of the dragon are one." Le Guin's view of language (or if you prefer, dragon's breath) aligns it with wind and possibility more than with writing and instruments of control. Which makes this a good place to reflect on the way that Earthsea's magic breaks through most directly into our own world in Le Guin's enchanting style, her inimitable way with words.

Style and Attention

Le Guin consistently stressed that a fantasy world must be unapologetically made up. Her brilliant essay on style in fantasy, "From Fairyland to Poughkeepsie," puts it like this:

> There is no borrowed reality of history, no current events, or just plain folks at home in Peyton Place. There is no comfortable matrix of the commonplace to substitute for the Imagination, … only a construct built in a void, with every joint and seam and nail exposed.[14]

She does not simply mean that below the visible boards of a fantasy world lies a subfloor. Her point is that the joints and seams and nails are *it*: Words are the world. What you read is what there is.

Take another look at how *A Wizard of Earthsea* begins:

> The island of Gont, a single mountain that lifts its peak a mile above the storm-racked Northeast Sea, is a land famous for wizards. From the towns in its high valleys and the ports on its dark narrow bays many a Gontishman has gone forth to serve the Lords of the Archipelago in their cities as wizard or mage, or, looking for adventure, to wander working magic from isle to isle of all Earthsea. Of these some say the greatest, and surely the greatest voyager, was the man called Sparrowhawk, who in his day became both dragonlord and Archmage. His life is told of in the *Deed of Ged* and in many songs, but this is a tale of the time before his fame, before the songs were made.[15]

Cather spoke of the novel as an empty room; that principle helps us understand how Le Guin's under-description sparks inference. I read the words—*goat bleats, storm, mountain behind clouds*—and I put myself to work as well. The abiding beauty of those sentences lies in the world it evokes. Out of "storm-racked ... high valleys ... dark narrow bays" of those opening chapters I conjured up as a child (and still do) a tangible, weather-worn world: storms at sea, early frost before the crops are harvested, goats pushing their way past the boy trying to mind them. Again that poem from Le Guin's version of the *Tao Te Ching* seems apt:

> Hollowed out,
> Clay makes a pot.
> Where the pot's not
> Is where it's useful.[16]

The words are the clay—but the pot gets made in the reader's mind

Tolkien's vision of "subcreation" (the author as a maker of "secondary worlds") presumes that readers *fall* into a world made of artfully arranged words: the second they start to question things, the music stops and the spell is broken.[17] That is not how Le Guin's writing works. Le Guin is interested in creating a world that becomes real to her readers not *despite* but *because* of its distance from our actual world. She is happy to have her readers notice how they are creating that island of Gont in their minds. She has rendered a scrupulously effective diagram—now readers can make it into a living picture.

Le Guin's commitment to concise evocation operates everywhere in her books. That's why the Miyazaki film, *Tales from Earthsea*, despite many flaws in its narrative structure, is such a delight: the animators took her prose and translated its world-building into pictures. However, reading Le Guin always inclines me to Tolkien's position: that there are powers of fantasy world-building reserved for the written word alone.[18] At the end of *Tombs of Atuan*, for example, Ged and Tenar sail into Havnor Great Port, returning the ring of Erreth-Akbe to its rightful home. But even as they enter, Tenar is taking strength from a further voyage they will be making. Ged has promised her that they can quit that noisy triumph for a quiet home in the hills of his home island, Gont:

> They came after the sunrise and the sunsets, the still days and the icy winds of their winter voyage, into the Inmost Sea. They sailed the crowded lands among great ships, up the Havnor Straits and into the bay that lies locked up in the heart of Havnor and across the bay to Havnor Great Port. They saw the white towers, and all the city white and radiant in snow. The roofs of the bridges and the red roofs of the houses were snow-covered, and the rigging of the hundred ships in the harbor glittered with ice in the winter sun. News of their coming had run ahead of them for Lookfar's patched red sail was known in those seas; a great crowd had gathered on the snowy quays and colored pennants cracked above the people in the bright, cold wind.[19]

If you are asking yourself how wind can be *bright* as well as *cold*, that question makes you just the reader Le Guin hopes for—and works to create. The brightness of the wind is of a piece with the cracking of the pennants and the snowiness of the quay: a Bruegel picture in words.

You might say that Le Guin works not to solve a scene but to render it. She wants you to have sensations a moment carries with it as well as its salient physical details. Often that means experiencing it alongside a voyager who, like the reader, comes to a place for the first time:

Tenar sat in the stern, erect, in her ragged cloak of black. She looked at the ring around her wrists, then at the crowded many-colored shore and the palaces and the high towers, She lifted up her right hand, and sunlight flashed on the silver of the ring. A cheer went out, faint and joyous, on the wind, over the restless water. Ged brought the boat in. A hundred hands reached to catch the rope he flung up to the mooring. He leapt up onto the pier and turned, holding his hand out to her. "Come!" he said smiling and she rose and came. Gravely she walked beside him up the white streets, of Havnor, holding his hand, like a child coming home.[20]

Tenar is *like* a child coming home. And yet readers do not lose sight for a minute of the fact that this is a new place to her. As "she rose and came"—Le Guin supplies both verbs where one might do, elongating the ceremonial quality of the action—she is neither coming home nor arriving where she wants to be. This moment has some sense of formal homecoming woven into it. Yet it is not an arrival, it is rather a protracted pause during a journey we know will continue beyond Havnor, at least as far as Gont. She, like the reader closing the book, is coming home and going away at once.

Attention

Le Guin style produces in the reader a kind of watchful waiting: you set yourself aside in favor of the impending and available world the writer lays before you. Simone Weil names this willful temporary self-forfeiture "attention."[21] It is akin to the power of passivity that lets the poet John Keats delight in a billiard ball by entering into its "roundness, smoothness, volubility and the rapidity of its motion." "If a Sparrow come before my window" he writes, he will "take part in its existence and pick about the gravel."[22] Attention in Weil's sense means an openness to those moments of exhilaration or transition or triumph.

I first became aware of how writing could produce that attention when reading Le Guin as a kid. I can pinpoint the sentence exactly. Early in *The Tombs of Atuan*, Tenar gets a visit from Penthe, virtually the only cheerful person in her world, who comes bearing apples. Tenar isn't hungry, but she urges her friend to eat one then and there: "Penthe selected the smallest, out of politeness, and ate it in about ten juicy skillful interested bites."[23] Even now, eating an apple I notice that I am taking *interested* bites, and (how could I make this up?) I find myself counting to see if a given apple is going to take me ten bites to finish. The sensation Le Guin creates for her readers is the antithesis of the well-rendered verisimilitude of a high-end video game. A line like "ten skillful juicy interested bites" floats free of its original context and alights, leaving a reader feeling that her world is very far away—and right here in the palm of a hand.

Looking for examples to supplement that lowly apple (I blushed at so trivial an object sticking in my mind so long), I opened *The Farthest Shore* at random. This kind of attention is truly everywhere: the first page I turned to depicted the young protagonist, Arren, running into a store to buy a present for his mother. The shop-keeper quotes a high price:

> "I can see you are a judge of the old crafts," said the shopkeeper, looking at the hilt—not the handsome sheath—of Arren's sword.[24]

And that redirection—check out the hilt of that sword we weren't even aware he was wearing—opens a lane for focused readerly attention. Rereading it now I recall, suddenly, how it struck me as a child, the questions it raised. Two paragraphs later, gift bought and ship in sight, Le Guin relieves the tension by training readers' eye on the sword as easily as she had shifted them to Penthe's apple:

> His father had given him the sword on the eve of his departure from Enlad ... For it was the sword of Serriadh who was the son of Morred and Elfarran; there was none older in the world except the sword of Erreth-Akebe, which was set atop the Tower of Kings in Havnor. The sword of Seriadh had never been laid away or hoarded up, but worn; yet was unworn by centuries, unweakened, because it had been forged with a great power of enchantment. From it, the great treasure of his family, Arren had received his use-name: Arrendek he had been called as a child, "the little Sword."[25]

Through these sentences (and others like them everywhere in the Earthsea books) run veins of older stories untold. Morred and Elfarran are one story, the Tower of Kings another. The story readers get instead, unexpectedly sneaking up on us because we followed this tangent, is the surprising origin of our hero's own name. Arren awkwardly catches his ankles against this inherited *arren* as he tries to stride manfully through the streets. Our attention is caught and anchored in the here-and-now of the incident—and yet it's also pointed backward to those other, lost stories that give substance to the hovering edges of the story-world.

If Le Guin achieves that sense of semi-detached immediacy on the level of the sentence, she also has other deeper ways of reaching readers where they live. It is Le Guin's sentences that first open up Earthsea. But something else keeps us there. It may be the granular tangibility of that made-up world—its uncanny capacity to be at once entirely magical and entirely material, at once enchanted and gritty. That brings us to her animals.

Actual and Ideal

Trust a goat ... to spoil anything.[26]

A tension runs through the Earthsea books: between the magical underpinnings that perennially remind readers of Earthsea's unreality and the vivid details that make it feel real. On the one hand, the magic Le Guin dreams up serves as reminder that we all live in the realm of ideas, memories and feelings, which flow through us and shape how we see the world. Yet concurrently we live in a completely tangible actual world, shaped by the rules of physics and biology. The perfect symbol of the human capacity to imagine the world differently, to think magically, is the dragon. And the countervailing symbol of the earth's earthiness is ... goats.

In *Tehanu* for instance (this is a case where the same basic pattern prevails from *A Wizard of Earthsea* all the way to *The Other Wind*) Tenar slips away briefly to mourn her dead mentor and father figure, whose name she learned just as he died. She is distraught, and her grief culminates in the involuntary exhalation of the most precious syllables that Earthsea holds, a wizard's true name:

> "Aihal!" she whispered.
> For answer a couple of goats bleated, out behind the milking shed, waiting for Heather to come. "Be-eh," one said, and the other, deeper, metallic, "Bla-ah! Bla-ah!"[27]

"Aihal" is sound elevated to its highest magical power. "Be-eh" (and I speak from experience here ...) is the blurt of a goat giving utterance to some intestinal distress, or maybe just pleading for attention. Le Guin's gloss on this moment—"trust a goat to spoil anything"—captures the tension perfectly. Tenar wishes she could be a world where one could simply have one's thoughts, and let them unfold in solitude. But she actually lives in a world where goats are there to echo—or rebut—any thought that crosses your lips.

Goats are spoilers in that they bring you back down to earth. Yet they are also enliveners, because they make the dream-world of fantasy suddenly tangible. The incongruity of mage's name and goat's bleat reminds me of Auden's 1938 "Musée des Beaux Arts." That poem too emphasizes how even the deepest and most consequential human interactions take place against a backdrop of domestic animals:

> That even the dreadful martyrdom must run its course
> Anyhow in a corner, some untidy spot
> Where the dogs go on with their doggy life and the tor-
> turer's horse
> Scratches its innocent behind on a tree.[28]

Auden's example is deliberately gruesome, while Le Guin's goats are faintly ridiculous. Yet both Auden and Le Guin are focused on an enduring doubleness. Even the most distinctively elevated or awe-inspiring human actions (in these cases, mourning or execution) take place in a world where all of us get itchy and feel the need to give utterance to our feelings. Bodies—which grow frail, and age, and fail to behave themselves according to our ideals— are inescapable. Even though magic may seem to offer a way to escape from the bodily facts of life, they unexpectedly return with a bleat.

Action and its Opposites

"Why do we do what we do?"[29]
"He has done with doing."[30]

Another aspect of life on Earthsea resembles that on Earth: the crucial distinction between cogitating and taking action. Does it seem inevitable that Le Guin's kind of quest fantasy should favor the actor over the contemplator, that fortune should favor the brave? Not exactly. In the earliest chapters of *A Wizard of Earthsea* Ogion tells the young Ged that even turning away a raincloud by wizardry can loose unintended consequences elsewhere. That every action has more drawbacks that rewards is a lesson Ged and every protagonist who follows has to learn slowly, repeatedly, the hard way.

It is plausible to see everything Le Guin is doing between 1968 and 1974 as part of science fiction's progressive—and very action-oriented—New Wave.[31] If you look back at her by way of Margaret Atwood (the influence of Le Guin on *A Handmaid's Tale* and other Atwood jeremiads is crystal clear) it is easy to see the spirit of straightforward *activist* protest that links Le Guin to roughly contemporaneous writers like Kurt Vonnegut, Joanna Russ, John Brunner, Octavia Butler, J. G. Ballard, and Samuel Delany. Le Guin unmistakably aligns herself with this optimistic bent toward energetic amelioration. She feels its tug.

Both in her science fiction and in Earthsea, young protagonists (and even the middle-aged Dr. Haber in *The Lathe of Heaven,* ever active, ever convinced of his own virtue) are certain that discovering a problem leaves them only half a step from naming and enacting a solution. By one reading, in fact, the Nixon-era Le Guin oeuvre is a litany of American misdeeds at home and abroad. Stop using religion as an occasion for Gothic confinement of women (*Tombs of Atuan*). Stop promising arrogantly that brain power and the accumulation of knowledge can cheat death (*Farthest Shore*). Stop bringing down the forests and also stop fighting unjust wars abroad: the slightly creaky and slightly preachy *Word for World Is Forest* combines those two messages in a Vietnam War / Agent Orange multiplot about a hi-tech (and transparently American) space-going society persecuting sweet arboreal aliens. Stop abusing one another inside the home: *The Beginning Place* has a lesson about that. You might even read *The Lathe of Heaven* alongside John Brunner's contemporaneous *Stand on Zanzibar* as an Ehrlich-style warning about the dangers of population explosion, with its final soothing vision of a cleaner and distinctly smaller Portland circled by salutary greenswards.[32]

Only there is a catch: even to undo in Le Guin is sometimes to overdo. The impulse to act, to make a difference, seems a *sine qua non* of the world of heroic fantasy. Yet it is actually something that Le Guin warns against from the very second that action in Earthsea begins. Even in the first Earthsea trilogy the quest plot is turned upside down; you might call it fable of undoing. In *A Wizard of Earthsea*, the first deed Ged manages is using enchanted fog figures to lead invading soldiers to their death, an ambiguous triumph. The second is to unleash a shadow, which then chases him over land and sea, seeking to take his soul completely. You can grasp what follows as heroism (I certainly did when I read the book at age nine): Ged chases the shadow, names it with his own name, owns it, merges with it, and vanquishes its power. All this looks wonderfully clear: action prompted by a sense of responsibility.

That action, though, is nothing more than an attempt, partially successful, to undo Ged's original misstep. The novel from about page fifty on can be understood as his attempt to leash that shadow again, to make the deed un-be.[33] Le Guin refers frequently to a wonderful epic of his later life that we readers never actually hear: *The Deed of Ged*. A better title for the novel we actually do have might be the *Misdeed of Ged*. Or—if you are willing to take its ending as a happy resolution rather than the pushing-off point for a further set of necessary doings and undoings unleashed by that primal act—*The Misdeed of Ged Undone*.

As a kid, I was trained always to be *doing* something. Preparation and watchful waiting was not enough. The world was filled with self-evident tasks to accomplish: set the table, take out trash, do some homework—and bask in the glow of merited praise. To call that way of thinking "decisionism" recognizes the psychological imperative it encodes: always act, and let the action make its own meaning.[34] It is dinnertime: pick chicken or beef. We are at war: join the army or the navy. Our enemies must be overcome: drop the bomb on Hiroshima or Nagasaki. Or both. J. Robert Oppenheimer reported that at the moment of the Los Alamos test detonation a line from the Bhagavad Gita suddenly came to mind: "Now I am become Death the Destroyer of Worlds."[35] Suddenly, because only at the end of the chain was he able to look back summatively at all those beautifully well-intentioned steps that took him, his country, his species, his world into the Nuclear Age. Decisionism's capacity to forestall reflection until a moment of branching paths undeniably arrives generates a sort of Zeno's paradox in reverse: no intermediate step seems to take you closer to the moment of choice—yet you do in fact arrive there.

Mired in the Anthropocene, we are all hard at work nowadays reckoning up our capacity to destroy our planet with a thousand different unintended consequences. In that work it is easy to feel very alone, convinced we face choices no earlier generation ever had to. But we can clearly trace a forerunner to that existential angst in the science fiction of the Atomic Age. Like Oppenheim himself the authors who reckoned with Hiroshima found themselves asking how the great and good intentions of scientific heroes like Einstein and Fermi, ardent to defeat Nazism, might end by delivering us to the most hellacious game-theory principle imaginable: mutually assured destruction.[36] The unintended consequences of well-intentioned scientific advances are the overt topic of novels like Nevil Shute's *On the Beach*, Mordecai Richwald's 1959 *Level Seven*, and Walter Miller's mid-1950s *A Canticle for Leibowitz*. They also make up a none-too-subtle undercurrent of novels from Aldous Huxley's *Ape and Essence* (1948) to Kurt Vonnegut's *Galapagos* (1985): endgames for humanity written in the shadow of the discovery that humanity has become the potential destroyer of its own world. To act is to obliterate.

Le Guin's resistance to the virtues of action and to pride in accomplishment goes equally deep. However, it has more complex philosophical roots. I have spent years thinking about where Le Guin fits in the story of fantasy and also in the realm of American writing at large. I don't shelve her with the angry satire of Mark Twain or Kurt Vonnegut. I love Twain's refusal, especially late in life, to lighten his dark diagnosis of American capitalism, consumerism, and complacency.[37] However, many readers of late Twain flinch away because they feel only the heat of his anger, not the light of his wit.

Le Guin belongs to a subtler, trickier tradition, one that seems to go along with the current of the day, smiling agreeably, while underneath working hard to push readers out to sea, into parts unknown.[38] C. L. R. James is right to see in Melville and Whitman hints of that American tradition of surface serenity and sub-surface wildness—Ralph Ellison's *Invisible Man* belongs there as well.

In a previous book, I praised some earlier American artists for their refusal to go along to get along.[39] One was Willa Cather, who looked at the apparent uniformity of Western prairie towns and saw they really contained endlessly various ways of living with and on that land, recombinations of many cultures (Native American, Spanish, Czech, German, Anglo) that met and mingled there. Another was Buster Keaton, who refused both the cheery conformity of Harold Lloyd and the complete world-refusal of Charlie Chaplin. Keaton always advanced into the world just half a step off the beat: he was not a square peg jammed into a round hole, but more like an octagonal one, the sort that looks like it really ought to curve right in, except for those loveably non-compliant corners.

I sense the same stubbornness in Le Guin and love her for it. In a series of essays about recalcitrance in *Public Books*, I praised Jean Stafford and Doris Lessing, writers of Le Guin's generation who made careers out of rejecting the dismal confines of what passed for suitably feminine roles in the blinkered middle of the American century. Stafford spends her career inventing alternatives to cocktail parties and the—sexist and racist—rules of the social game. Stafford, though, can only imagine her antisocial alternative as austere, internal, unpopulated, and impossible. Lessing takes resistance a step further: she denies that social rules bind us the way we think they do, and she offers up a frequently impolitic vision of ways to stand apart from the flow of coercive empathy and misleading sympathy. If Stafford thinks to herself "I'm in Hell," Lessing tells the rest of the world to go there.

Le Guin's struggle is a subtler one. She turns that specific and historically contingent question around the Atom Bomb (*will we blow ourselves up?*) into a comprehensive accounting of the problems that arise simply from assuming that the main function and virtue of human life is to act, act, act.[40] The earliest spell that Ged casts costs the lives of men who are attacking his town: men who came to kill, yes, but his action kills them in their turn. And the first significant spell he casts, the first act of real wizardry is to summon up a shadow (the *gebbeth*, the doppelgänger) that becomes his first and worst enemy, scarring him and sending him on a book-long quest. A quest, when all is said and done, simply to un-make that original action.

Her heroes and heroines come onto the scene all primed up to act—and their first steps invariably lead them astray. Not because they are bad-natured or misguided, but because all unconsidered actions summon up shadows. Ged is lucky enough to get the chance to face down the gebbeth he unleashed in the world with his first great acts. The rest of us can spend a lifetime looking for the right step backward, the un-do button that never appears:

> I, who am old, who have done what I must do, who stand in the daylight facing my own death, the end of all possibility, I know that there is only one power that is real and worth the having. And that is the power not to take, but to accept. [41]

And beyond that mistrust of acting lies a deeper one still: acting *in concert*. Le Guin mistrusts the action even of one person acting without sufficient deliberation. How much more must she fear anything undertaken under instruction, or "only following orders"? Her avowedly anarchist politics shape her resistance to allowing any leader to take charge of the body politic as a whole. And they explain one of her most curious semantic distinctions: even if you want to call her fantasy works novels, don't tell Le Guin they have a plot. For her, it's *story* all the way down.

Not Plot but Story

> Actually I'm terrible at plotting, so all I do is sort of put people in motion and they go around in circles and they generally end up where they started out. That's a Le Guin plot. I admire real plotting, but I seem not able to achieve it.[42]

It took me a long time to grasp Le Guin's warning about the thirst for action, that juvenile impulse that sent me and countless other 1970s children to Greek myths and to adventure science fiction. One reason I was slow to grasp her desire to divert that impulse is that Le Guin is not the sort of writer who negates, who wants readers to feel bad for being themselves. Her work is not a stop sign, it is a side door that suddenly opens. For all her distrust of action for action's sake, Le Guin spoke to the wanderlust in me as well. What she loved was stories, and islands for those stories to take place on. And characters on the move.

It is a long fantasy tradition, the island-hop: William Morris's *Water of the Wondrous Isles* is a gem, and Lewis's *Voyage of the Dawn Treader* follows unabashed in his footsteps. But there is a special twist in Le Guin: perambulation turns out to be the one kind of action that Le Guin wholeheartedly embraces.

The fantasy novelist is first and foremost not a plotter but a world-maker. Lest you think this is an overly metaphysical point, it is worth noticing it is one that Le Guin herself makes—and from a couple of vantage points. She clearly has in mind from the first the strangeness as well as the irresistible allure of world-creation: the ways in which it represents the fulfillment of a basic human dream, and also the sort of hubris and vainglory it risks engendering. I am not going to say a lot in this book about the day I traveled to Portland to meet Le Guin herself. But I'll never forget her glee explaining that the first stage of creating Earthsea was "literally [to] sit down and draw a big map with lots of islands, about which I knew nothing at that point. I named them, happily. For the rest of the six books I could just travel around and find out what they were like."[43]

This is an underappreciated aspect of Le Guin's cosmology: the power it allots to storytelling, to bringing the meaning of events into view by bringing them *back* to life. In our interview, Le Guin distinguished between the brilliant intricacy of a Dickensian plot, all whirring interconnected pieces, and the mere brute incidence of *story*, events that simply happened to happen somewhere and sometime. "The story's where I go" is as good a manifesto as any for Le Guin.

There are always more stories in Le Guin, stories that defy any attempt to seal the novel's edges and resolve all its diverse occurrences into a single well-ordered machine. And a crucial implication of Le Guin's anarchist commitment to story over plot is that centers never hold. Le Guin admires the intricate connections Dickens builds between seemingly unrelated parts of *Bleak House*, but the stories that fill her books attest to her sense that life, even whatever life resides in literary characters, has a way of refusing the neatness that plot demands.[44]

Le Guin also makes a darker point about the godlike arrogance associated with this power to conjure up a new reality with words. It's not axiomatic with her to praise the creator, the one who can become (as Kipling put it in *Kim*) a "dreamer whose dreams have come true."[45] At one point late in *The Lathe of Heaven* (which Le Guin wrote just as she was finishing the first Earthsea trilogy), the well-intentioned but hubristic Dr. Haber reflects on what it means simply to dream new facts into being:

> A week ago, he had not been the Director of the Oregon Oneiro-logical Institute, because there had been no Institute. Ever since last Friday, there had been an Institute for the last eighteen months. And he had been its founder and director.[46]

The problem with Dr. Haber's calling up a new world is the sort of serene faith it requires in one's own power to know what's right; this is another version of the Le Guin warning about action and its always unknown consequences. One that must apply to herself just as it does to Dr. Haber.

Creation-as-hubris is the potent threat to Le Guin's deep-seated faith in the creative imagination. That tension adds an almost paradoxical twist to her Taoism: How can she preach the virtues of inaction, of restraint to the point of stillness, of being hollow like a pot, while still busily "subcreating" worlds into being? There is also a political way to formulate this problem: How can we go on exploring, discovering, and creating without becoming colonizers, without robbing others of their land?

From Taoism Le Guin takes an appreciation for *inaction* in the face of the nonheroic and downright humdrum responsibilities of daily life. That lends itself to a philosophy of restraint, an unwillingness to make people line up behind one. There is something like the paradox of an anarchist politics at play here: If you oppose government precisely because you are leery of its power to mobilize, then what sort of structure can your political mobilization take? If what you write is about the danger of acting so as to persuade and change others, then what exactly do you see your own writing doing?

Le Guin's most consistent response to this tension is to create what we might call a *non-territorialized space* within her books
themselves. Make the act of discovery imaginative and perhaps
imagination can prevent spoliation. Put another way, maybe the
inventedness of the fantasy world can prevent Le Guin's form
of action (making up fantasy worlds) from precipitating malignant real-life disasters engendered by Dr. Haber's world-rewriting.
Samuel Delany was the first novelist to deploy Michel Foucault's
notion of the heterotopia: in 1976 he named a novel *Trouble on Triton: An Ambiguous Heterotopia*.[47] But Le Guin too turns her novels
into heterotopias: that is, spaces within yet apart from the rules
and regulations of "normal" society—like cemeteries, prisons,
and bordellos. "The New Atlantis" (I praised its beauty briefly in
the Introduction) puts this process into our own world by having
a new island rise off the coast of Oregon. The eruption of that new
island stands in for the imaginative act always available to readers
as it is to Le Guin the writer. If this world distresses you, head off
into the imaginative realm to conjure up another.

Not *The* World, A World

Le Guin, then, lets readers glimpse some of the most polarizing
questions in present-day society from another perspective. Shelley's account of the value of poetry speaks of the "transvaluation of
value" that comes about inside an artwork: that is, the aesthetic as a
space where the highest ethical work is done not by promulgating
a particular ethical stance, but by putting stances in conversation
with one another, letting the reader evaluate them outside of the
present moment.

Le Guin's fantasy transports its readers to a world not governed according to our rules. Our usual empirical shortcuts are out of bounds here. In Earthsea somebody really may turn from man to bird, the dead really may come back. Dragons exist, speak, reveal their kinship with people. All operates according to its own logic—a logic that the reader does not make sense of within the world as is, but within a world apart, one wrought by the author.

In her 1994 afterword to *A Wizard of Earthsea*, Le Guin apologizes for falling into fairy-tale logic. I love the nature of that apology. It is not for extravagant or excessive invention, but for *not going far enough* in making things up:

> The stories [I was immersed in as a child] weren't about the women. They were about men, what men did, and what was important to men. It's in this sense that *A Wizard* was perfectly conventional. The hero does what a man is supposed to do: he uses his strength, wits, and courage to rise from humble beginnings to great fame and power, in a world where women are secondary, a man's world.[48]

That is, she has no problem with showing us the world as it cannot be. Her only regret is the extent to which she relied on time-worn (Western, patriarchal, bigoted) well-trodden fairy-tale paths. Suspending belief properly means putting all such tracks aside.

There is a remarkable distinction Erich Auerbach makes that I often think about. In *Mimesis*, he describes the way that the Old Testament established the reality of its world and the characters moving within it, by way of the story of Abraham's journey with Isaac. Details are obscure, motivations elude us, and somehow all of that half-sketched information triggers a sort of infilling on the part of the reader, Auerbach says. We find ourselves thinking ourselves into the situation, which we accordingly assume and come to believe is happening in *the* world, the only one there is, inhabited alike by Abraham and by readers. By contrast, the perfectly illuminated world of Homer's *Odyssey* is clearly set apart and away from us. The characters live in another world: it may be marvelous or terrible, desirable or horrific, but is simply *that* world over there, where they live like that. Plausibility doesn't enter into it—in the way that it might for example with Abraham's decision to sacrifice Isaac—because they order things differently there.[49]

Tolkien once defended himself against the accusation of writing allegorical fantasy—he was always touchy about Middle Earth being confused with Narnia.[50] Nothing here is an *allegory*, he insisted—but it remains possible to *apply* what you see in that world to what we experience in our own. Those are two ways to characterize fantasy worlds—or perhaps better to say two ways to characterize their effect on readers. If you follow Auerbach, you stress the appeal of that brightly lit space apart, the world over there. If you follow Tolkien, the essence of the effect lies in the application—in readers' capacity to map that world onto our own.

When I think about Le Guin, both approaches ring true. Her world, every joint and seam and nail of it, floats up there in the sky. And yet that very separation is what invites me to apply whatever I've gleaned about her characters' lives to my own. I measure the gap—then impetuously jump into their shoes. That made it all the more striking to me two decades after *The Farthest Shore*, when Le Guin appeared in Earthsea once again—changing the rules, the characters, and just what it meant to jump.

Figure 4 Michelangelo's "Dragon and Other Sketches" (*c.*1520–30; item 15190), © Ashmolean Museum, University of Oxford.

CHAPTER 3

EARTHSEA REVISITED

It's been a joy to me to go back to Earthsea and find it still there,
entirely familiar and yet changed and still changing.[1]

It would be easy to praise Le Guin's work indiscriminately. But I
don't think she would thank me. The day I clambered up a hilly
Portland street to meet her, she ended the interview by leading me
down into her pleasantly musty basement to select books for my
kids. It felt—and feels even more now—like stepping down into
the Underworld. I vividly recall her beaming beside hulking metal
shelves of books, inviting me to choose. Well, I will.

In fact, I've already chosen once: when I wrote about her for *Public Books*, I focused on Le Guin as the muse of the Nixon era: *The
Left Hand of Darkness, The Lathe of Heaven, The Dispossessed*, and the
first *Earthsea* trilogy all came out between 1968 and 1974. Her anarchist aesthetics offered the beleaguered Left—not to mention the
beleaguered center—a vision of an *unmobilized* America, a country whose strength lay in its slowness to act, in its suspicion of
patriotic fervor.[2] In recalcitrance, hope.

Le Guin's death, though, taught me to think again about what
happened after that brief span. If Fitzgerald had been right about
there being no second acts in American lives, those seven years
would have been plenty. Only, he wasn't—which also means
I wasn't. Two decades later, Le Guin began publishing Earthsea

fiction again. In *Tehanu*, *Tales from Earthsea*, and *The Other Wind* she told it all over again, only different.

In that second trilogy, Le Guin added stories that revealed hidden aspects of her world—and hidden weaknesses. In the first trilogy, Earthsea's essence rested on three inviolable rules: that magic's power "consists in ... the true naming of a thing" in "True Speech"; that there is perpetual enmity between deceitful, morally ambiguous humans and truthful but irredeemably deadly dragons; and that wizardry and the School of Wizards on Roke is strictly a boys' club—everything else is "weak as women's magic ... wicked as women's magic."[3]

All three of those earlier Earthsea rules, however, turn out to be a misunderstood inheritance, belief-generating stories that had hardened over generations into seemingly inescapable laws. (I am sure Le Guin loved "It is a truth universally acknowledged ..." Jane Austen's sly opening line about perfectly obvious truisms that turn out to be anything but universal and anything but true.)[4] The later Earthsea books are not inversions, but rotations. Everything that had been mapped with *x-y* coordinates is now also measured along *z*, a previously invisible axis.

This chapter is an appreciation of how she opens up that new line of sight, that third axis. On another level, it is an appreciation of how all literature, perhaps especially fantasy, can always be adding an axis to readers' view of the world. And it points toward the final chapter of this book, where I reflect on what that added dimension meant for *me*, what it showed me about the blinkered way I had read—and even lived.

Scholars can and should argue about what allowed Le Guin to revise and resubmit Earthsea. Did the ferociously gender-blind feminism that inspired *The Left Hand of Darkness* spur Le Guin to disavow the implicit quest machismo of *A Wizard of Earthsea*? Did her turn toward Taoism persuade her that inaction is the silent and often the better partner of action? Whatever the answer, what matters most to me is the boldness with which she turned a cold eye, a dragon's searching eye, back on the comfortable green world she herself had made decades earlier. If she can do it, why can't we?

Full of Meaning …

To be a Le Guin reader is to become accustomed to thinking on your feet, and to noticing the impermanence of even the most self-evident and seemingly immutable things:

> Several black stones eighteen or twenty feet high stuck up like huge fingers out of the earth. Once the eye saw them it kept returning to them. They stood there full of meaning, and yet there was no saying what they meant. There were nine of them. One stood straight, the others leaned more or less, two had fallen. They were crusted with gray and orange lichen as if splotched with paint, all but one, which was naked and black, with a dull gloss to it. It was smooth to the touch, but on the others, under the crust of lichen, vague carvings could be seen, or felt with the fingers—shapes, signs. These nine stones were the Tombs of Atuan.[5]

Full of meaning, and yet there was no saying what they meant; that sums up just about everything readers come across in Le Guin. You believe in her novels as a world apart, yet also find yourself struggling to relate that world to your own life. A double exposure.

One of the core insights in Le Guin's writing, reiterated in different forms, is this tension between the world's bare bones and the world that we construct out of our shared impressions. She is interested in the flesh that we add to the world's bones, the ways we put together our own impressions and the stories we have been told all our lives, the things we accept simply because those around us are persuaded they are true (according to Friedrich Nietzsche, "truths are illusions which we have forgotten are illusions"). The "Yes … and" game that Le Guin plays in the later Earthsea books takes into account the fact that wizards use the Old Speech—but adds the fact that dragons somehow *are* that speech. It takes into account that humans and dragons are antithetical beings, but adds the fact that they arose from the same root stock. It takes into account the fact that after death the disembodied souls of Hardic people (Ged and those born on the western islands) cross into the dry timeless Land of the Dead. But it adds the fact that after death Kargish people (those born on Earthsea's eastern islands) undergo the same fate as nonhuman animals: their soul dissolves like their body and their atoms are reborn into a different living form. Fantasy may remain true to its previously revealed rules, yet allow for the unfurling of new possibilities.

"Weak as Woman's Magic"

In *Tehanu*, Le Guin takes aim at a sexist set of ideas about life and magical powers present in Earthsea from the beginning. Present, of course, because placed there by Le Guin herself. But that does not mean she feels it incumbent on herself to defend them. Memorably, Tenar reflects on the way she was taught to understand the work of witches, when compared to the power wielded by mages or wizards: "*Weak as woman's magic, wicked as woman's magic,* she had heard said a hundred times."[6] The phrase rankles with Le

Guin because its repetition means something: an adage reiterated long enough to be believed can actually make itself into a practical truth.

In the second trilogy, Le Guin wants readers to see why women's magic has long been called weak and wicked on Earthsea: because it had potency and a virtue all its own, and because there were men who wanted that knowledge hidden away.[7] The phrase stands revealed as of those "pictures that held us captive" Wittgenstein wrote about. By failing to perceive, or laboring to forget, an obvious fact of life—women's equal capacity to learn, and hence to practice powerful and good magic—those who repeat the phrase actually create the very condition they bemoan or despise or warn against. This is not nearly as simple as Le Guin saying, *the old adage is wrong*. Rather she is showing how an adage like that can become right; by structuring the lives of those men and women who grow up hearing it. It should come as no surprise to the careful reader of Le Guin's Earthsea books that "The Finder," the lengthy novella that kicks off *Tales from Earthsea*, goes back to the origins of Roke and reveals that the school for wizards was founded by women with magical powers. The original exclusion of women from Roke, and all the sneers and bigotry that follow from that apartheid, came about not because woman's magic was "weak," but in a strenuous male reaction to its potency.

Le Guin's notion—that adages become true in practice by dint of repetition and belief—suggests that world-building is not just something that a few special writers with far-ranging imaginations get to do in the moment they sit down to write about a world like Earthsea. Instead, little imagined worlds that become true by dint of being repeated and believed are born around us every day. We are all making up Earthseas, we are all complicit in their continued fantastical life. Life does not just imitate art—it turns out that life itself *is* art. In our everyday actions we too are creating such worlds, made up of lies whose falsity has been forgotten. I can't help thinking about the final page of George Eliot's *Middlemarch*: "But we insignificant people with our daily words and acts are preparing the lives of many Dorotheas, some of which may present a far sadder sacrifice than that of the Dorothea whose story we know."[8] With *Tehanu*, Le Guin moves to make explicit what had only hovered beneath the surface of the first three books. Fantasy pertains to real life not because fantasy is real, but because reality is fantasy.

Trauma and Therru

> It's so easy, she thought with rage, it's so easy for Handy to take the sunlight from her, take the ship and the King and her child-hood from her, and it's so hard to give them back! A year I've spent trying to give them back to her, and with one touch he takes them and throws them away. And what good does it do him—what's his prize, his power? Is power that—an emptiness?[9]

Tehanu is the most painful Earthsea book. By a long way. It feels painful even to write about it, which may be part of Le Guin's point. This is a story about the knotted side of life, the back of the tapestry. At its grimmest—the horrific early pages in which Tenar adopts the burned and abused child Therru after Handy has left her for dead—you might even call it an anti-story. That is, its power lies in depicting someone frozen into a wounded moment, incapable of undoing that wound or getting beyond it. This being Le Guin, the wound is given a physical form: the terrible burning that closes one of Therru's eyes and makes one arm into a claw. But readers understand the burn in a deeper way as well.

Viewed in this way, the passage above about the abuser Handy's capacity to "take the sunlight" from Therru when he reemerges signals Le Guin's acknowledgment that genuine trauma can't simply be nudged back into the narrative world. A reality-altering wound cannot be made a manageable piece of the past by some piece of narrative sleight of hand.[10]

Trauma in Earthsea is real, and acknowledged. Its purest case, this burning of Therru, leaves an indelible horrific scar. For Tenar to be asked on the first page of *Tehanu* "why do we do what we do?" is not simply to reopen the question that shaped the first trilogy: Is action ever justified? It yokes that question to this most horrific instance of the durable afterlife of a moment—a child beaten, then thrown into the fire in an attempt to cover up the beating.[11]

Trauma is the frozen afterburn of that single action. Tehanu's scars are the ephemeral heat of that flame locked into time forever, always marking how hot, how deadly that flame was in that one instant her face met it:

> There was [because of the abuse Therru had endured] a gap, a void, a gulf, on beyond the right and the truth. Love, her love for Therru and Therru's for her, made a bridge across that gap, a bridge of spiderweb, but love did not fill or close it. Nothing did that.[12]

By burning her, Handy moves Therru into the realm of imaginary timelessness, where the past event comes back and holds onto her so tightly that it no longer even seems to belong to the past. Her suffering actually invokes another kind of timelessness: the deathless eternity sought by the wizard Cobb in *The Farthest*

Shore. Trauma then is on some deeper level akin to the kind of timelessness of experience that we *think* we wish for ourselves.

The wounding of Therru suggests that Le Guin, two decades on, is ready to reckon as the earlier books had not with the durable harm that can come about in everyday life—as a direct result of ordinary ignorance, callousness, sexism, and indifference to gendered violence. In the first trilogy, such events can all eventually be mastered narratively. As Isak Dinesen put it (and Hannah Arendt never tired of repeating) "All sorrows can be born if you put them into a story or tell a story about them."[13] In the first trilogy, Le Guin represents artworks—stories, epics, sagas, songs, even "deeds"—as orderly and legible and rational. More than that, she shows them restoring what we might call story-order to Earthsea. By contrast, *Tehanu* explores, with evident reluctance, the possibility that certain wounds, certain evil, may resist such amelioration by way of story.

May resist, not *must*: Tenar herself survives an assault at one point, and finds the next day that it still seems to be occurring to her. She, temporarily like Therru, is immobilized by the awfulness of what happened. However, that horror does not last. Tenar (there are advantages to adulthood, after all) knows that making a story of it will allow her to put it, in various senses of the word, *behind* her:

> Friends from the village came by all day long to tell and be told … She found that their company revived her, carried her away from the constant presence of last night's terror, little by little, till she could begin to look back on it as something that had happened, not something that was happening, must always be happening to her.[14]

That is the same spirit of narrative recovery that thrilled me as a child reading the first Earthsea trilogy.

It is also clear, though, that the novel contains problems—like the irremediable harm done to the burned Therru—potentially beyond the capacity of storytelling to heal or to change. Trauma theorists have many names for the out-of-timeness that can descend with trauma. But Le Guin is not wrong to think of trauma's quintessence as its capacity to freeze things, to turn the ongoingness of the world into a burning empty moment. Nor is she wrong to compare living forever (a promise made by various power-mad wizards in Earthsea) with the horrific fate that Handy inflicts on Therru: both arrest time unnaturally, and destructively. Therru is forced to live, half-burned, inside the single moment of the wounding, to carry it always with her as something actually happening now.

The "tell and be told" Tenar establishes with her friends is what allows her to know what happened as a fact of the past tense.[15] For Therru, by contrast, the traumatic event suspends sequence and makes the replacement of one moment by another impossible. W. B. Yeats expressed a related thought about the dangers of immobility in "Easter 1916," his poem about political martyrdom during the Irish Rebellion. Its most quoted line—"a terrible beauty is born" doesn't shed much light, but another does: "too long a sacrifice can make a stone of the heart." The core of the poem is the stanza devoted to explaining what it actually means for sacrifice to turn a formerly beating heart into unyielding stone:

> Hearts with one purpose alone
> Through summer and winter seem
> Enchanted to a stone
> To trouble the living stream.

The horse that comes from the road,
The rider, the birds that range
From cloud to tumbling cloud,
Minute by minute they change;
A shadow of cloud on the stream
Changes minute by minute;
A horse-hoof slides on the brim,
And a horse plashes within it;
The long-legged moor-hens dive,
And hens to moor-cocks call;
Minute by minute they live:
The stone's in the midst of all.[16]

The point is that martyrdom's steadfastness is not valor but a kind of terrible frozenness, like the lifelessness of rocks. Or the terrible immobility of the burned half of Therru's body, where that original crash into the fire is always ongoing.

In *The Other Wind* too there is a broken character who seems frozen by his wounding: Alder, whose loss of his wife has left him permanently moored in his dreams to the wall that separates the living and the dead. Like Therru, he can seek solace but there is no remedy for his loss—all he can do is register and make sense of a life permanently defined by that one terrible fact. So are we to think that Le Guin fully embraces "the trauma plot"?[17] Is it hearts frozen to stone all the way down?

Le Guin herself, in "Earthsea Revisioned" acknowledges the capacity of violence to wreak what seems to be inescapable trauma. However, she also names a way to transcend that wound: the wildness of dragons:

> The dragon Kalessin ... is wildness seen not only as dangerous beauty but as dangerous anger. The fire of the dragon ... meets the fire of human rage, the cruel anger of the weak ... and consumes it,

for "a wrong that cannot be repaired must be transcended." There's no way to repair or undo what was done to the child and so there must be *a way to go on from there*. It can't be a plain and easy way. It involves a leap. It involves flying. So the dragon is subversion, revolution, change … It is the wildness of the spirit and of the earth, uprising against misrule.[18]

The horrific violence wrought on Therru in *Tehanu* seems to be blocking the story, enchanting Therru to a stone in that immobilizing way Yeats describes.

However, dragons are the wildness and uprising that starts motion again. Should we read the arrival of dragons as simply a magical and hence imaginary solution to a real problem? Yes. And No. The ways in which Le Guin tests the powers of fantasy against such real pain as Therru's are central to the second trilogy's accomplishments. *Tehanu* shows how mightily Le Guin struggles against trauma—not because she does not value it properly, but precisely because she does.

Elaine Scarry proposes in *Body in Pain* that pain takes away language, leaving a space of primal because unverbalized experience.[19] The harsh whisper with which Therru makes herself barely audible even to those who love her best might seem a marker of just such unvoicing. However, Le Guin also sees that thickened harsh whisper as a necessary component of Therru's growth. Suffering may not ennoble but neither does it freeze; it educates, given the right chance.[20]

On the very same page of *Tehanu* on which we find Tenar raging against Handy because of the pain he has inflicted on Therru, she also encounters Ged's young pupil Arren—who will become King under his true name, Lebannen. She finds that "her heart yearned toward him." Why? Because he has suffered with Ged on their shared quest and found himself deeply wounded with him as well. Tenar pays tribute to the suffering—that he knows what it is to be hurt, and therefore to know what others feel when they too are wounded:

> He thought he had learned pain, but he would learn it again and again, all his life, and forget none of it.[21]

This notion of learning and relearning offers one way out of trauma. Even the immobilized loop of recurrent suffering, retold for another's benefit, is restored to the cathartic frame of narrative.

I ultimately see in Le Guin what I admire in Hannah Arendt— the insistence that story will out. Eventually all kind of timeless-ness, from immortality to trauma, have to be supplanted by the endless tick-tock of the universe, and by the indomitable human desire to verbalize time passing, to turn mere succession into comprehensible sequence. For Arendt the key story in question is the almost (but not quite) unspeakable horrors of the Holocaust.[22] For Le Guin it is the endlessly ramified and inventive capacity of humans to inflict pain on one another. Both notice at the core of the worst kinds of evil an attempt to suppress the truth about their occurrence, to silence those who bear direct witness to atrocity.

Kurt Vonnegut opens *Slaughterhouse Five* by noticing what it means to try to write about trauma when one is too close to the site of the wound: "Lot's wife looked back at her city and was turned into a pillar of salt. This is a novel written by a pillar of salt."[23] The burned child Therru also threatens to become one: it is not just her scar that is repeatedly described as frozen or immo-bile, it is Therru herself. Once she can recover the side of her that is not human but dragon, though, she is free to fly on "the other wind."

Coming Unstuck in Space and Time: Dragon/People

> In Tenar's Earthsea there's neither acclaim nor reward; the out-
> comes of actions are complex and obscure.[24]

There is a medieval notion that an angel may be better than a rock,
but a rock and an angel are still superior to two angels. Call it the
multiplicity principle: it partially explains the appeal of dragons.
In them Le Guin finds the promise of some unimaginably distant form of life generally glimpsed riding far aloft on "the other
wind"—but capable of plunging from the sky to call you by your
name, perhaps once in your life.[25]

In *Tehanu*, although both Ged and Tenar have leading roles to
play, the central figure is unmistakably the burned and abused
Therru. By the book's end she has found her true name (it is also
the book's name, Tehanu) and has discovered within herself both
a human and a dragon nature. She is the burned victim of childhood abuse, but also the child of dragons; hence in touch with the
wild powers of the earth. Her dragon aspect lies outside human
society and its rules, and it acts according to a rough justice that's
swift and inhuman. When Therru calls to them, her dragon-kin
arrive, burning various malefactors (not just her original attacker)
to ashes.

What does Le Guin mean to show her readers here? Merely that
one lucky human in a generation has dragon nature buried within
her? Something more. Because she was so horribly burned at age
six, Tehanu eventually discovers what lies nascent within all of
us: the dragon side of human nature. We are all both dragon and
human, both wild and tamed. However, most of us live and die
never glimpsing that doubleness. Only when the world shapes and
strikes us in just the right way—and only if we stand ready to tell

the story that makes sense of that shaping, that striking—is our natural doubleness revealed:

> [Dragons] speak the Language of the Making, in the knowledge of which our art and power lies. They are beasts as we are beasts. Men are animals that speak.[26]

> "Once Sparrowhawk said to me ... that the dragon and the dragon's speech are one thing, one being. That a dragon does not learn the Old Speech, but is it."[27]

Just as she was completing the first Earthsea trilogy, Le Guin published the essay I mentioned earlier, "Why Are Americans Afraid of Dragons?" Her answer is blunt: "We tend, as a people, to look upon all works of the imagination either as suspect, or as contemptible." Meditating on those dragons that she wants Americans neither to fear nor to ignore, she concludes that

> fantasy ... isn't factual, but it is true. Children know that ... by such beautiful non-facts [as "once upon a time there was a dragon"] we fantastic human beings may arrive, in our peculiar fashion, at the truth.[28]

That all looks like a much more moderate defense of dragons than her fiction provides. Le Guin seems to be saying that our belief in such non-facts as the existence of dragons is what makes us human? Only, there is one word still needs explaining: "we *fantastic* human beings."

What is it that makes humans as fantastic as dragons are? Answering that sheds light on what makes Le Guin's imagination at once so appealingly childlike and also so deep, so old, so unsettling. True, dragons are invented out of the whole cloth, out of wherever stories come from. So too on some important level are human beings. We too are notional and definitional: Does humanity begin at birth? At language acquisition? With the Neanderthals? With *Homo habilis* and all the other big-brained primates who shared the earth before *Homo sapiens*? With men alone? With adults alone? Le Guin's sneaky point is not simply that humans are "fantastic" in our essence, but that essence itself is fantastical. It is nothing but lies (better, nothing but stories) all the way down.

In the later Earthsea books Le Guin rolls out a resonant new metaphor for making sense of the innately and unavoidably fantastical nature of human life: the two-sided artwork. Early in *Tehanu*, Tenar goes to visit the workshop of an old weaver who is called Fan, after a beautiful antique fan given to his grandfather by a grateful client:

> It was displayed open on the wall. The delicately painted men and women in their gorgeous robes of rose and jade and azure, the towers and bridges and banners of Havnor Great Port, were all familiar to Tenar as soon as she saw the fan again.

Now Fan asks her, "Did I ever show you the other side of it?" Flipped over, the fan reveals a scene in which dragons rather than people are the central figures:

> Dragons moved as the folds of the fan moved. Painted faint and fine on the yellowed silk, dragons of pale red, blue, green moved and grouped, as the figures on the other side were grouped, among clouds and mountain peaks.

But the scene on one side and the scene on the other are related:

> "Hold it up to the light," said old Fan. She did so, and saw the two sides, the two paintings, made one by the light flowing through the silk, so that the clouds and peaks were the towers of the city, and the

men and women were winged, and the dragons looked with human eyes.

"You see?"

"I see," she murmured.

Le Guin highlights that lesson again when Tenar puts the fan back up on the wall. She "remounted it as it had been, the dragons hidden in darkness, the men and women walking in the light of day."[29]

There is an 1854 entry in Thoreau's journal lamenting the fact that his home state, Massachusetts, had allowed the preacher Anthony Burns, successfully escaped from slavery, to be sent back to Virginia in shackles. It is a horrific epiphany for Thoreau: he realizes that his own active participation in civic life, his taxes, and all the rest, actually went not to building a free society, but to buttressing and upholding a slave one:

> Suppose you have a small library, with pictures to adorn the walls — a garden laid out around — and contemplate scientific and literary pursuits, &c, &c, and discover suddenly that your villa, with all its contents, is located in hell, and that the justice of the peace is one of the devil's angels, has a cloven foot and a forked tail — do not these things suddenly lose their value in your eyes?[30]

That thought experiment is a gothic one—like the movie *Get Out*, it challenges readers to recognize the uncanny in their own seemingly placid lives[31].

Le Guin's Earthsea works instead by carefully triangulating readers' experience through another world. It may feel like reality to the characters, but to readers its invented nature is clear. Still, when Le Guin turns the screw on her Earthsea, I feel the same lurch that Thoreau wanted readers to feel. Those enemies we feared turn out to be us, in another guise. When Le Guin first asked why Americans were afraid of dragons, the answer seemed to be that we fear to confront the imaginative alternative to our humdrum reality. But a better way of putting it might be that we fear to confront the fact that our humdrum reality is itself an act of imagination.

As I was finishing this book, I discovered *The Dawn of Everything*, in which David Wengrow and David Graeber set out to show how various, and complex, and utterly unpredictable different human social forms have been.[32] They are arguing against all teleological evolutionary models of human societies working their way "up" through inevitable stages. That "stadal" theory was around more than two centuries ago in Rousseau and in his Scottish Enlightenment counterparts, but different versions—which feature small primitive bands of hunter-gatherers succeeded by farmers and then inevitably by kings and their enslaved minions of peons— crop up nowadays in pattern-finders like Jared Diamond and Juval Hariri. Wengrow and Graeber see infinite possible living arrangements. That monarchy, or slavery or monotheism happens to flourish in one city and wither in another is to them less upward climb than a kind of lottery randomness. There is perpetual change, but no telos, no evolution from the simple to the complex, or the brutish to the beautiful. It is imagination, and invention, all the way down.

I suggested earlier that we think of the second Earthsea trilogy as adding a new axis to the world of Earthsea: making a flat painting into a sculpture, you might say. In the Victorian mathematical fantasy *Flatland* the arrival of a Sphere makes the protagonist ("A Square") realize that there is more to life than his normal two-dimensional senses enable him to perceive.[33] The metaphor of the axis, then, suggests that there is another dimension to human life as well if only we could raise our eyes and catch sight of it: we are all Squares, and life would be better if we could think spherically instead.

The metaphor of the dragons and humans inhabiting the same fan-space, sharing the very same eyes, is something a bit more intimate and jarring. We need not look away to discover the dragons, this metaphor suggests. All along, our dragon selves have been right there with us. In Edith Wharton's *House of Mirth*, as Lily Bart begins her sad descent from New York's aristocracy to its working class, she finds that she still sees certain wealthy people from her old days in high society. But now she glimpses them from below. Wharton's metaphor is unforgettable: "Lily had an odd sense of being behind the social tapestry, on the side where the threads were knotted and the loose ends hung."[34] Wharton is emphasizing the difference between what Erving Goffman called "front stage" and "back stage" self-presentation.[35]

Le Guin, too, is referring to an essential quality of humanity that is kept hidden. We tell ourselves the dragons are foes, but in truth they are just another side of us, hidden on the back surface. The metaphors have a slightly different valence, but each writer is exposing an omnipresent sort of human blindness, the failure to recognize how intimately the back and front sides of the same surface are tied to one another. Each makes a point about art's capacity to shed light on both sides, to compel its audience to grapple with the doubleness that is universally present, but so easy to ignore.

Le Guin is offering her readers, accustomed to think of dragons as villains on the edge of human society, a new way of understanding what it means to be a thinking being. Peter Godfrey Smith's *Other Minds* argues that although octopuses think complexly and playfully, just as humans do, they do not think *like* we do. Le Guin's dragons are imaginary, unlike octopuses: understanding either, though, requires an imaginative investment on the observer's part. Hannah Arendt defined "representative thinking" as the ability to take on another's ideas, to enter into what their convictions and impressions must seem like from the inside. She had neither octopuses nor dragons in mind. Thanks to speculators like Godfrey Smith and Le Guin the moment she described—"one trains one's imagination to go visiting"—*can* be extended to both the fantastical and the invertebrate.[36]

In the foreboding early 1930s, Walter Benjamin memorably diagnosed "left melancholy" in the poetry of Erich Kastner.[37] Ursula Le Guin strikes me as an instance, perhaps the best one we have, of that melancholy's antithesis. Le Guin embraces the multiplicity of stories and the multiplicity of viewpoints on those stories, not weakly but strongly. The only way to see the world is all the ways. And the only way to keep those various ways alive is to practice respect, tolerance, and most of all an expansive interest in the standpoint of others. One learns to think as others do, to internalize their views and hence to enlarge one's own. That is a left-wing politics that relies on art to help us cross the gaps. And it is hopeful: not optimistic perhaps, but inevitably and relentlessly hopeful. What other choice do we have?

Story upon Story upon Story

The second Earthsea trilogy's new thought about dragons—they are fantasy creatures who reveal just how fantastical we humans also are—goes hand in glove with a new Le Guin idea about the interaction between individual stories and the larger story-world in which they occur. In the first trilogy, Le Guin manifested her appreciation for *story* (individual peripatetic action across an open-ended seas of islands) over *plot* (the neat coincidence-fuelled tightness of a Dickens novel). In her final three Earthsea books, however, she begins to explore ways that stories can converge, coincide, overlap, and generally come together in fortuitous ways. Rather than lapsing back into Dickensian plot, she offers a new way to think about those fortuitous moments when different stories happen to converge, or to collide.

When Le Guin says that the beauty of her islanded Earthsea is that it allows her to simply move from place to place, she sells the second trilogy short in one crucial way. That description makes it sound as if a Le Guin book is primarily a single story line that rambles or drifts its way from island to island, randomly accreting experience. Even *The Tombs of Atuan* foreshadows the way that, in her later Earthsea books, story meets story in haphazard but profoundly influential ways. Thomas Hardy refers to this sort of unpredictable coming together of events as "hap" and the word resonates with the sort of story Le Guin tells.[38] In *Tombs*, Ged's quest for the bracelet of Erreth-Akbe happens to intersect with Tenar's coming of age. Her leap-of-faith decision to help him is the crucial turning point in her life. It also happens to be the key to Ged's long peripatetic quest. Taken together, those two outcomes eventually lead to a reunion between the long-divided Hardic and Kargish lands.[39]

By the second trilogy, the power of sheer contingency to bring together multiple story lines is fully established. In both *Tehanu* and *The Other Wind*—and equally in "Dragon-fly," the short story from *Tales of Earthsea* that Le Guin called a "bridge" between *Tehanu* and *The Other Wind*—the pattern of story-meets-story intensifies. In *The Other Wind*, there are three separate plotlines: the dragons from the West are moving rapidly eastwards toward the heart of Earthsea; the Kargish princess Seserakh arrives from the East, forcing Lebannen to decide if he will marry her and form a Hardic/Kargish unity; the humble mender Alder is troubled by dreams of his dead wife reaching out to him over the wall that separates the living from the Land of the Dead. Simultaneous incursions from the West, East, and Underworld—and for much of the book no hint of the pattern that might emerge out of those diverse stories.

In all three works, an older wisdom figure comes to realize that a seemingly trivial affair among "ordinary people" (generally female) is subtly linked to what seem to be central and surpassingly important affairs (always dominated by men) at the story's seeming center. In *Tehanu* there is a prophecy about the importance of finding "a woman on Gont"; at first nobody connects that prophecy to the small withered Therru. In "Dragon-fly" the trivial disturbance is a girl who wants to enter the male-only Roke school for wizards at the same time that the magic-addled Summoner is trying to extend the sway of death over the land of the living. In each text, there is a period in which the connections between those peripheral (female, small) and metropolitan (male, large) stories is far from evident. The resolution in each case lies not within any single story, but in the contingent relationship that emerges *between* the stories. It is the intersection of one small life with another at just the right moment that makes great things happen.

The Other Wind marks the most fully developed version of the convergence of small stories into large outcomes. The arrival of the Kargish princess Seserakh seems to be a story about "bartering of brides." It is much more: in what at first seems a trivial episode, that seemingly abject bride-to-be tells Lebannen and the Roke wizards a crucial piece of Kargish lore, which uncovers the unity between dragons and humans. And then there is a small-time magician Alder, an insomniac "healer of pots."[40] His discovery that he can hear his wife's voice over the wall between the Living and the Dead signals the waning of an old magic that had demarcated a place "beyond the west" for the souls of humans. By finding a way to allow the dead to die, Alder becomes the modest linchpin of the story that reunites the Kargish and Hardic lands (in a love match) and also allows the dragons to restore proper wildness to the western lands. Furthermore, beneath it all–a resolution that can only arise from this convergence–is the revelation that has been "hiding in plain sight" from the beginning of the series. The underlying commonality between dragon and human (who have long inhabited opposite sides of the fan) becomes visible again. The convergence of these three plots suddenly enables both dragons and humans to grasp and acknowledge the ancestral link. All that arises from sheer syzygy: the burned girl Therru, the pot-healer Alden, and an unwilling Seserakh arriving in Havnor. Arriving and proceeding to do things nobody expected of them—things they had not even expected of themselves.

It is tempting to say that this convergence of multiple stories has been present in Le Guin's Earthsea from the beginning—since the result of *The Other Wind* is to make sense of all six books as part of a single tapestry. However, I think it is truer to the spirit of her own creation to mark the way that Le Guin's thinking about the power of stories developed over the years. She uncovered an appreciation of the complex interactions caused by the fact we individual humans are born sharing a world with others whose own particular stories are developing along their own respective timelines. On the one hand, Le Guin's account of Earthsea has never been about kings and leaders and gods: no one individual has the right or authority to make their story an inevitable part of some larger pattern. On the other hand, individual stories can converge with one another, in unpredictable ways that can form complex emergent patterns. Girls become dragons, pot-healers become wall-breakers, and people fall in love. In *The Other Wind*, those three events occurring together is enough to change the world.

One final point about Le Guin's decision to return to the world of Earthsea and take a look behind the tapestry, so as to see the dragons with the human eyes. In 2021, the novelist Howard Norman sent me his memories of a dinner at Le Guin's house in Portland. Someone asked:

> "If you could change or extend a memorable or iconic story, how would you do that?" And I remember Ursula Le Guin spinning a most wonderful new ending for the classic Billy Goat's Gruff children's story … the Troll, while, yes, being knocked into a river or fast-moving stream, in fact ends up in a downriver or downstream little village, where the Troll starts a bakery! In her new version, the Troll was certainly depicted as an "outsider" or marginalized figure, who proves himself indispensable to the community. [41]

Like Huck Finn, Le Guin's troll lit out for the territories and reset the story. By altering its locale it also altered its reputation, its character, even its moral nature.

That anecdote says a lot about Le Guin as a rewriter, someone who likes nothing better than moving around in what Salman Rushdie calls "the ocean of story." It also says something about Le

Guin's decision to reopen the case of Earthsea after a long silence. It is not so hard to play the game of adapting fairy tales to the present day, and only a little harder to imagine what happens to these characters as they enter the happy or miserable "ever after." When Le Guin turns back to her own characters—turning the magic-less Ged and widowed Tenar into unlikely parent figures for a younger generation—something trickier is afoot. By returning to the world she herself wrought, and revealing surprising hollow places where solid ground had seemed to be, Le Guin is reminding readers how much of the world consists in the stories we tell about it.

Stepping back into Earthsea a generation later, Le Guin is writing about a generation that no longer takes for granted what went without saying: the land of the dead, the power of names, the Old Ones, women's exclusion from wizardry. "Over ... All changed!"

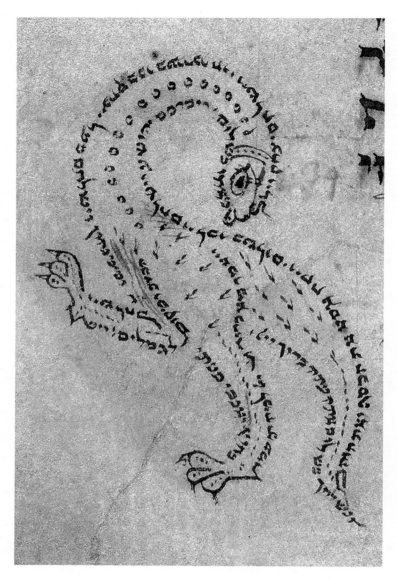

Figure 5 "Textual micrography" drawn from the British Library's Yonah Pentateuch (Add MSS 21160; c. 1300–99). The Polonsky Foundation Catalogue of Digitised Hebrew Manuscripts.

CHAPTER 4

MY EARTHSEA

The dragons of Earthsea remain mysterious to me.[1]

Writing about Earthsea has forced me to think hard about an innately boring subject: my middle-aged self. I'll have a bit more to say below about the childhood that preceded it, but for now it's enough to say that Philip Larkin has a suitable line to sum it up: "Nothing, like something, has to happen somewhere." As far as my adulthood goes, aside from a few anecdotes about raising chickens in Boston, the report is even less remarkable. When the Manager in Conrad's *Heart of Darkness* says, "Men who come out here should have no entrails," he might have been looking for Plotzes.[2]

But even the most sedate stream has a current, complete with eddies, backwaters, and the occasional snag. Le Guin is my map for all of that—not because I picked this assignment, but because she has taught me how to think about the course of a life. What it owes to fate, to origins, and to the people met on the way, whose way of being and seeing alters everything. In *Middlemarch*, George Eliot has a slightly chilling observation about how the actual paths our lives take deviate from their planned trajectories:

> For in the multitude of middle-aged men who go about their vocations in a daily course ... the story of their coming to be shapen after

the average and fit to be packed by the gross, is hardly ever told even in their consciousness; for perhaps their ardor in generous unpaid toil cooled as imperceptibly as the ardor of other youthful loves, till one day their earlier self walked like a ghost in its old home and made the new furniture ghastly. Nothing in the world more subtle than the process of their gradual change![3]

What exactly does it mean to sense a youthful impulse walking like a ghost inside one's adult body? What happens when an earlier thought reemerges years later, and finds itself terribly out of place inside the new mental architecture that has sprung up in the meantime? "Even in their consciousness" adults learn not to ask that question, for fear the answer will throw them off the neat new rails they've built for their present career.

One of the satisfactions of novels that bear rereading (*Middlemarch* and the Earthsea books rank high on my list) is that they force the reader to confront that "subtle ... change" and figure out what to make of it. When I was eleven at summer camp in the woods of New Hampshire, I knew for sure I wanted to be a professional archer. Although I still feel that he's me, that I am him, I shudder to think what that future archer would say, waking up in Brookline, with eczema, children, pets, and a slushy winter-morning commute. Eliot calls such midlife collisions with long-ago dreams "ghastly." She has a point: the ghost of our own past selves is hard to exorcise.

Trace this book's origins, then, to a moment when I realized that the impulse that brought me into the classroom had been transformed subtly over the years, without my openly acknowledging it. I looked at the way my syllabi had changed over the years—first William Morris and Lewis Carroll quietly replacing Dickens, then a new twentieth-century lineup: Stella Benson and J. R. R. Tolkien followed by Naomi Mitchison, Philip K. Dick, Le Guin. It made me ask myself why fantasy had started to seem realer to me than realism.

I read *A Wizard of Earthsea* to my daughter when she was six. We were curled up on her bed in a shack behind a friend's rented summer house. It was dark outside, the bedside light was a cozy yellow and she leaned in as I read the words that carved a deep furrow into six-year-old me:

> The island of Gont, a single mountain that lifts its peak a mile above the storm-racked Northeast Sea, is a land famous for wizards.

It's lodged in my memory for good reason. That summer was the last time she ever let me read Le Guin to her. We made it through *A Wizard of Earthsea* and (captive audience) started on *The Tombs of Atuan*. But once we got into the underground, those dark scary caves where Ged was chained, she wanted out, into the daylight. No matter how many times I brought Le Guin back in subsequent years, that ban stayed in place. Plenty of things we foist or try to foist on our children tell us about the childhood self we are trying to recapture. This is not Daria's story, and Le Guin is not her writer. The real question is not why my kids didn't want to read *The Tombs of Atuan*, but why I suddenly did.

There is a seemingly satisfactory answer: because I loved teaching undergraduate classes on fantasy and science fiction. Students showed up early, did the reading and then some, asked for permission to design their own games and enlist their classmates as roleplayers. However, crediting the class is putting the cart before the horse. What strange spirit from before my teenage years told me to reread Le Guin? What even stranger spirit made me cry again at the end of *The Farthest Shore*, when Ged stands broken on the far shores of the land of the Dead, his magic powers gone and nothing but a sharp-edged black pebble to show for it? What was going on with me that her world still seemed bright with promise to me, while so much else in our country was going dark?

There is a lot to say about the sense of childhood that surged up in me as I reread. Before that, though, an adult point: I love writing a book about Le Guin, but it also makes me deeply ashamed. As many people have said to me—some politely, some enviously, some censoriously—2023 is a funny year to turn back to Earthsea. My credo has been that Le Guin offers more than the sort of aesthetic escape that Arendt dismissively calls an oasis. If you listen to her right, I tell them (and myself) she offers a response to many of the woes of the world at large—ethno-nationalism, climate change, the ever-increasing American wealth gap.

Still, I've struggled at times to say that and mean it. The last half-decade has frequently had me sidestepping academic firefights I wasn't expecting. It is not new to hear university administrators urging humanities professors to be *relevant* and to train students in the valuable skills required in the professional world. Newer, though, was a message I began to hear from colleagues I respected and liked trading ideas with. I started to feel pressure to design classes to make students into better people, or to make sure they got engaged in the right kind of politics. I understand that desire to change the world by direct action. If you are pretty sure what's right, and what young people ought to enter the world primed to do, why not let them know?

Only how exactly is a teacher supposed to relate that concept of direct action to what happens in a classroom? I found myself thinking a lot about Le Guin's Dr. Haber in *The Lathe of Heaven*.

Like an overly confident professor, he takes charge of the reluctant dreamer, George Orr, and starts issuing him instructions for how to dream the world differently. They are all great instructions— only they come with unintended consequences. *Get rid of racial hatred!*—he dreams everyone gray. *Bring peace between nations!*— there is an extraterrestrial invasion. *Solve overpopulation!*—a plague kills 90 percent of humanity. Faced with Dr. Haber's righteous mission, George (another character aptly dubs him "Mr Either/Orr") struggles impressively *not* to put his world-changing powers to work.[4] In fact, it's George's hesitancy, his distrust of action, that saves both him and the world.

That rang true to me. I have always seen the classroom as a place where students could draw breath for a while without wondering what each breath was for. It is important to find a way to slow the heart, steady the eyesight, recalibrate the hearing. If my students could enter and reflect on the worlds built by novelists— Eliot, Woolf, Cather, Ellison—I thought they'd return to our own with a sense of what matters to them, and to the no-longer-so-mysterious other people around them.

I went through some Dr. Haber-ish years myself, thinking that raw anger, rawly expressed, could shame the adult world (especially my parents) into lockstep with my own views. At eighteen, I thought spending three nights in a lean-to on the steps of my university library would convince our administration to divest from South Africa. A couple of years later, though, my temporary gig in Vaclav Havel's newly free Czechoslovakia was teaching English at Camp Brontosaurus, up in the acid-rained Krkonoše mountains of western Czechoslovakia. There I found myself struggling with tensions that sometimes felt like impossible contradictions. My students were environmental activists—which didn't stop them subsisting mainly on cans of cold pork. They also worshipped Ronald Reagan, and loved learning words like "networking" and "interface." Even then, I remember grappling with the implications of giving them what they wanted. Did teaching them to speak and read English so they could subscribe to the *Wall Street Journal* make me an agent of neoliberalism?

When I moved to San Francisco in search of a job, I was still in my shouting years. My year as assistant editor at Michael Lerner's *Tikkun* made for further spiritual struggles. My editorial assignment was to clarify and simplify articles that preached socialist domestic politics (good by me); but I was also put in charge of rewriting editorials that endorsed George Bush's "surgical strikes" against Iraq (not so good). What exactly was my responsibility about those pieces, which appeared under someone else's byline but were made up of words that I had rearranged—or even proposed to writers myself? That was when something started to shift for me—when I started to see George Orr's point about thinking more, doing less. Maybe my own shouting could wait, while I hunted down comma splices and split infinitives. Clear expression had an ethics all its own. By putting something into a form where others could agree or disagree, writers might wake in readers a recognition of narrowness in how they saw the world.

When I arrived in graduate school after *Tikkun*, a lot of my time was still spent among the reds, or at least the pinks. My dissertation was aimed at vindicating the kind of "proletarian consciousness" that Marxists like Georg Lukacs praised. I wanted to explore how activists like the mid-Victorian Chartists developed a new theory and practice of "crowd power." How much longer could I pretend my parents were my enemies, though, if I was following my mother not only into graduate school but also into the study of nineteenth-century literature?[5] I even took a course with her beloved teacher David Perkins, a shy sweetheart of a man who lived and breathed Romantic poetry.[6] The home my mother had found in the 1960s, I found again in the 1990s.

I realized how happy I was to be in the classroom—preferably seated at a long oval table where we could all splay our books open to the same page, glancing downward as we talked. To judge means grasping your own grounds for judgment: developing a way of reading that lets you recognize your prejudices, your assumptions, most of all your blindnesses. That was when it began to seem to me that the classroom was not where students got taught right and wrong. Instead, it was a place they went so they could learn how best to decide for themselves. Le Guin had a part in all that, somehow. She was one of those who shaped the pot I poured myself into.

Mobilizing for Action

The year I revisited Earthsea in earnest, though, was not 1991 but 2016. When my science fiction students read 1984 the week Trump got elected, they had no interest in fiction as an oasis: here was Big Brother staring them straight in the face. I may have turned to speculative fiction because reality was heating up beyond my comfort zone, but it turned out that the appeal of speculative fiction had nothing to do with escaping reality. Students wanted tools they could use to diagnose and change that reality.

Writing the section of Chapter 2 that analyzes Le Guin's opposition to action, I recognized in myself at my students' age a strong version of the impulse that she was warning against. As a child of the 1980s, of Reagan's America, I was brought up always to be doing, to measure my worth by how much work I'd accomplished. To make my résumé the measure of my life. Like many of my generation, for a long time that ethos served me well. You find something you love to study: that was poetry, briefly archery, until it was chess, until it was Latin, until it was a summer of fruit-fly genetics that I don't talk about much ... You plow your furrow deep to put a crop in the ground. That the furrow remains after the crop has come and gone is an idea I came to only later. If you had asked me then about every action's unintended consequences then I might have admitted that I wasn't even sure about the intention behind the shortest of short-term consequences.

What if I had been a better reader of Le Guin back then? If I had noticed that Ged's first spell (cloud figures to lure soldiers on) was fatal, his second (summoning a wraith) required all his teacher's prowess to undo, his third (same kind of misguided summons) cost another teacher's life. Maybe that way of looking at Ged would have allowed me to admit that taking a temporary teaching job in Prague was something a lot more significant than an "educational opportunity." Yet that's what I remember earnestly calling it, in an expensive international call to my parents. Maybe I would have reflected more on the possible resemblances between me and Jeff and Jeff, my two American housemates who walked around small Moravian villages with stacks of $100 bills in their shoes ("in case I get a shot to buy anything ... maybe a church?"). Maybe whatever it was I struck up with Dana and Martin in Prague would have been less about "having Czech friends" and more about, well, friendship.

That earlier hyperactive John, according to George Eliot, is still haunting me, along with the would-be professional archer with acne and headgear. If I look for a reason to go easy on him (and of course I do) I remind myself that young John was prey to the quintessential Le Guin impulse: wanderlust. What I failed to admit to myself back then was that all this motion—to England, to Prague, to San Francisco, back to grad school in Boston—was less about doing doing doing than it was a way of turning orienting circles, the way a homing pigeon does a quick spin upward on release. I had no idea of my heading, but I knew I loved that gyre.

"Sufficiently Typical of my Class"

There are quick ghosts that haunt us, though, and then there are slow ones. When I turn back to Le Guin with a smile and a sigh of relief, that has something to do with the present-day battles I am ignoring—and it has to do with my sense of a Le Guin-less young adulthood wasted in pursuit of action. But it also relates to an earlier me who wanted simply to live in other worlds. The whisper that tempts me to write about Le Guin comes from 1975, from the second floor of my local library, where they turned on the fluorescent overheads and left you alone all afternoon.

Taking this adult look back at my naïve childhood reading was always going to be a problem. How am I supposed to make sense of the way that all those little scraps and memories taxi randomly back to me? In a late poem, Thomas Hardy hopes that his mourners will remember him principally for what "he used to notice": the "dewfall-hawk … crossing the shades to alight | Upon the wind-warped upland thorn" and the "nocturnal blackness, mothy and warm."⁷ So, a portrait of the artist as a young noticer. But here is a funny thing about my own effort to ape Hardy: the things I noticed about Le Guin as a child are inextricably bound up with where I was when I did that noticing. Telling the story of Ged travelling through Earthsea means trying to convey the scratchy green carpet in the front hall of our house on Livingston Street, where the sunlight poured through the screen door. How many thousand books did I read there, rolling onto my left side to read the right-hand pages, then back on my right to read the left-hand side?

Coming back to Le Guin as an adult, realizing how many sentences from her sank into me ("ten skillful juicy interested bites") forced me to reflect on what kind of kid I must have been for that writing to work on me as it did. One of my favorite recent writing assignments was an *in memoriam* for another Portland writer: Beverly Cleary.⁸ I realized while writing it that my admiration for her account of an unremarkable 1970s Portland childhood was mainly due to my own experience of a comparable Washington one. When I set out to write about Le Guin—and Le Guin's vision of what fantasy could do for her readers—I knew that my own childhood memories belonged to the story.

In the self-examination section of *Road to Wigan Pier*, George Orwell explains that to describe Wigan miners he also has to disclose some facts about his own more genteel upbringing, by virtue of their "symptomatic importance."⁹ So that readers can properly evaluate where his own work is coming from, Orwell does his best to disclose what he grew up thinking of as what goes without saying. Likewise, I am sketching my own childhood here as a way of disclosing the lines of force (*ley lines*, they call them in witchcraft) that may connect my love of Earthsea right back to my mother's dissertation on Romanticism, or my grandmother's poetry anthologies—about teaching, about math and science, about America.[10]

And yet those lines never run perfectly straight. How about exploring another kind of "symptomatic importance" in my love for Le Guin? I have now spent some time exploring what it meant for Le Guin herself to start examining Earthsea along a new axis, turning the flat painting into a three-dimensional sculpture. Or— to borrow her own metaphor from that dragon/human fan—to flip a painting over and reveal the always present but previously hidden other side. In Le Guin's Earthsea, understandings are constantly getting upended. Dragons go from mysterious hostile presences at the edge of the world to protagonists; the line between life and death goes from salvation to mistakes; the antagonism between warring peoples turns out to have been founded on a lie that, being uncovered, dissolves. "We had the experience but missed the meaning."[11] William Morris—an inspiration to Le Guin[12]—frames the thought in more revolutionary terms: "Men fight and lose the battle, and the thing that they fought for comes about in spite of their defeat, and when it comes turns out not to be what they meant, and other men have to fight for what they meant under another name."[13]

In that spirit, I think that same set of facts about my Le Guin-reading childhood might be framed entirely differently. Why did I need another world? Why was I so eager for the other side of the picture, where the dragons look back at you out of their human eyes? I am aware—perhaps increasingly aware the farther I move away from childhood—that throwing yourself into books also means throwing yourself out of something else. Leah Price calls it "reader's block": turning to books principally as a shield against unwelcome aspects of the all-too-actual world around oneself.[14]

There is a Victorian painting (James Tissot's "Room Overlooking the Harbour") that shows a married couple at breakfast, each apparently so deeply engrossed in their respective reading that to see the painting is to grasp instantly how hard they are working at ignoring one another.

When I was busy sharing a world with Ged, Tenar, and Le Guin herself, it never occurred to me to ask what that immersion had to with the world I was avoiding. I am sure it occurred to my parents. I paid attention to Earthsea; instead of what, exactly? Book-smart can mean world-stupid. There is a hillside next to the Deal Junior High playground I still pass with a shiver, remembering the lonely recesses and lunch hours I spent up there with a book, while ninth-grade life went on a few feet below. To that I could probably add a few hundred kick-the-can games I gave up for trips to the library; not to mention Jim Levin and Peter Berkowitz loafing in the basement poolroom at the community center, no more than 50 feet from my ratty library beanbag.

Unable to see myself clearly within my own world—were Jim and Peter my friends? Did I know how to act like a friend to them?—I sought a world where comfort came with the territory. Instead of having to look around me, and see what looks came back my way, I could focus on a hero or heroine—someone who didn't need to return my gaze, and in any case was already me beneath the skin.

Le Guin knew all about this human need, especially this childish need, to find that other world where things feel simpler for the reader—even if they are not especially simple for the characters depicted. "We have inhabited both the actual and the imaginary realms for a long time" is one way she expresses her awareness that kids like me in 1975 might have good reasons to seek imaginary solutions to their real problems.[15] Or to their reality problem.

There was loneliness in that childhood, there was silence, there were days when shyness overtook me. And there were times when my atavism, my inability to master the social patter of the playground and free play of more sociable kids made me into quite a jerk: my brother has forgiven my unintended cruelty, but that doesn't mean he has forgotten. Things are better for me now than they were for that shy and bookish kid who shuttled between Lafayette elementary school and the Chevy Chase library. Yet I still think of myself as living both in the actual and imaginary realms. I do still want to make fantasy my second home; and I think that Orwell would find "symptomatic importance" in that.

I can't forget that for whatever reason my parents and my teachers and even my long-suffering brother kept faith with me, which meant keeping faith with my inward exile, my absence. My childhood left me free to go away, to dwell in impossibility as if it were real. How hard it must have been for my parents to see me curling up into Earthsea, curling away from them, from friendship, from baseball, from all the solid substance that our actual DC neighborhood could offer—and did offer David. All this time later, I'm ready to come back and report on what I saw and felt. In letting me slip away to Earthsea my parents saved something special for me. Something that could have dropped out of my life and vanished.

Amor mundi

That brings us to the question of why my love for Le Guin persisted into adulthood. Not a simple one to answer. One way to begin: *For*

Love of the World is the subtitle of Elisabeth Young-Bruehl's biography of Hannah Arendt; that's her translation of *amor mundi*, a phrase Arendt loved.[16] Let's love *this* world, Arendt meant, rather than some imagined next one. Forget the ineffable or the imaginary: that way lies religion, and metaphysics and mystical handwaving that might as well be witchcraft. Take a look around you, take this one in, and be content. Almost always, that way of thinking satisfies me. I love Arendt's inspiring commitment to a here-and-now that is built both out of the physical world and the concepts by which we grasp it. Built out of our stories and memories and the knowledge that the other people around us also live with their own such memories: that we need to respect *who* others are rather than deciding *what* they are.

All my love for this world in the sense Arendt intends it—for goats, for the ocean, even for coffee—translates into a sweeping distrust of any kind of capital-B Belief that goes beyond rational knowledge of our own universe. Ever since my reluctant bar-mitzvah, my presumption has generally been against organized religion. Without wading here into the rights and wrongs of any one manifestation of organized religion (Zionism, homophobia, what have you) maybe I can stipulate that one thing I truly dread is a religious establishment's impulse to treat authorized *belief* as if it were a form of *knowledge*. It is one thing to present gorgeous parables in your houses of worship—quite another to take them as a bedrock reality. Fighting clear of the sort of religion that cruelly imposed its beliefs (not just where you eat and live, but who you love, what you do with your body) I found few things more dangerous than someone pretending that their sanctioned conviction had any more basis than somebody else's clashing credo.

And yet. My favorite books growing up were about witches and wizards, and those stories certainly required a very special kind of belief. I've clearly spent a lifetime admiring the power to call worlds into being with nothing more than words. In short, I loved belief, because I loved believing in something I could not see—so long as it was wrapped up in covers, and came with *The End* printed in large definitive characters on the final page. For a long time I felt sure that "believing" in Earthsea had nothing in common with religious belief; it made sense to me Le Guin described herself as "irredeemably secular."[17] Fantasy brags that it is made up—it always has.

Lucian of Samosata's *True Story* may be the first fantasy novel. Even two millennia after it was written, its opening words captures something deep about how fantasists think:

> I had no true story to relate since nothing worth mentioning had ever happened to me; and consequently I turned to romancing myself. But I am much more sensible about it than others are, for I will say one thing that is true, and that is that I am a liar.[18]

Displaying a sign that reads "includes lies" right at a book's outset is crucial, says Lucian. Because I only say out loud what every other writer knows but keeps quiet about: I'm inventing. You might even say that fantasy has the same relationship to religious belief that Judith Butler says "queerness" plays in relationship to "normative sexuality." Both strike the naïve viewer at first as the fake copy of a real original; in reality, though, both are fake copies of an equally fake original.[19] You might also put it even more baldly: the truth that fantasy brings to the table is precisely the lie at the heart of religion. All of that is a good reason to keep my belief in fantasy far apart from whatever religion has to say about the world: Le Guin's picture can seemingly never hold us captive, because she never tires of reminding us that it is, in fact, a picture.

I began this book by praising Le Guin for showing us that seeming truths can pass away the moment people realize that they are actually fictions. But in closing I think it is also worth praising her for a very different ability: not to disenchant capitalism, but to re-enchant mere words. In the medieval church, after all, mere cold facts were not miraculous: belief in the *im*possible is what makes a miracle.[20] Is that kind of belief in the thing you know can't possibly be true (a resurrection after crucifixion, say) so very different from my own passionate investment in spellwords and in Le Guin's dragons?

You may respond that "believing" in fantasy is nothing like believing in God—or capitalism. My belief in Le Guin's dragons takes place within the realm of "willed suspension of disbelief" and accordingly comes with an asterisk. You won't find me muttering Earthsea spells when the wind goes against me, or calling goats using their true name in the Old Speech. But I wonder if we might put the question of believing in Earthsea somewhat differently. Le Guin's dragons, wizards, and magical names are all purely fictional, sure. But when readers put their minds to that world, and ask themselves how it would be to live there, rather than here, aren't they sending their thoughts down a fresh pathway, which in turn opens up new vantages, new possibilities, new ways to disbelieve in what seems so natural to us here and now?

It did not take *The Dawn of Everything* to persuade me that none of the thousands of human societies that have actually flourished somewhere on Earth has the same social rules, beliefs, and practices as any other society. The work that Le Guin did on my childhood imagination already had persuaded me that the combination and recombination of beliefs, ideas, and facts about the world will never end—that our own world too, just like Earthsea, had to be imagined.

Love this world, surely. It is the only one we've got. But loving it properly also means jostling and smoothing it every now and then, so that its surface can realign, so that new patterns can emerge. If you believe in that, then isn't fantasy worth celebrating in the same way we celebrate other texts that solicit belief rather than providing empirical evidence? Isn't our willingness to enter the world where dragons, humans, and goats coexist something very like what Le Guin says it would mean to start disbelieving in the divine right of kings, or in capitalism? A crack in the smooth cosmos overhead, letting in a new kind of light. Making a new planet visible.

NOTES

Introduction

1 Le Guin, *The Books of Earthsea*, 984–5.
2 Le Guin, *The Books of Earthsea*, 7.
3 Tolkien, *The Monsters and the Critics and Other Essays.*
4 Plotz, *Semi-Detached.*
5 Parts of this paragraph adapted from Plotz, "Le Guin's Anarchist Aesthetics."
6 Wittgenstein, *Philosophical Investigations*, 115.
7 Le Guin, "Acceptance Speech—The National Book Foundation Medal for Distinguished Contribution to American Letters."
8 Arendt, *The Human Condition*, 8.
9 Kroeber, *Ishi in Two Worlds; a Biography of the Last Wild Indian in North America.*
10 Le Guin, *The Dispossessed*, 338.
11 Le Guin, *The New Atlantis and Other Novellas of Science Fiction.*
12 Le Guin, *The Books of Earthsea*, 559.
13 "Archaic Torso of Apollo," in Rilke, *Ahead of All Parting.*
14 "A portal fantasy is simply a fantastic world entered through a portal ... the fantastic is on the other side and does not 'leak'" (Mendlesohn, *Rhetorics of Fantasy*, xix). Le Guin does have one novel featuring a portal from the American Midwest into a fantasy world, *The Beginning Place*. Le Guin, *The Beginning Place.*
15 At first, this vision of Penthe in all her unapologetic defiance, her distance from Tenar's vision of herself and her future life, is flatly terrifying: "She did not understand. She felt that she had never seen Penthe before, never looked at her and seen her, round and full of life and juice as one of her apples ... She was scared by the solidity of Penthe's unfaith. Scared, she struck out" (Le Guin, *The Books of Earthsea*, 166).
16 In *The Dispossessed*, for instance, also written around this time, that "planet" is Annares, the moon (inhabited by anarchists) that orbits

the capitalist world Urras. In "New Atlantis" it's a new-old island that mysteriously emerges off the Oregon coast. What Tenar discovers here, Le Guin returns to in a hundred different ways: the world is more various than you know, and every time you really grasp a different way of understanding it, it is *as if* the world itself were reborn. The beauty of fantasy (and to some what makes it maddening) is its capacity to literalize that rebirth. In *The Lathe of Heaven*, the *Groundhog Day* of Le Guin fiction, George Orr sleeps and dreams the world differently over and over again. Maybe that is Le Guin's way of reflecting on what novelists do, each time they conjure a possible world into being.

17 But now at last the sacred influence
Of light appears, and from the walls of heaven
Shoots far into the bosom of dim night
A glimmering dawn; here nature first begins
Her farthest verge, and Chaos to retire
As from her outmost works a broken foe
With tumult less and with less hostile din,
That Satan with less toil, and now with ease
Wafts on the calmer wave by dubious light
And like a weather-beaten vessel holds
Gladly the port, though shrouds and tackle torn;
Or in the emptier waste, resembling air,
Weighs his spread wings, at leisure to behold
Far off the empyreal heaven, extended wide
In circuit, undetermined square or round,
With opal towers and battlements adorned
Of living sapphire, once his native seat;
And fast by hanging in a golden chain
This pendent world, in bigness as a star
Of smallest magnitude close by the moon.
(Paradise Lost, Book 2)

18 Le Guin, *The Books of Earthsea*, 558.
19 Laozi, *Tao Te Ching*, 14.
20 Cather, "The Novel Démeublé."

Chapter 1

1 Le Guin, "Why Are Americans Afraid of Dragons?" 38–40.

2 Williamson, *The Evolution of Modern Fantasy*, ix. Another example proving Williamson's point about Ballantine marking or creating a birth/rebirth of adult fantasy: Jill Paton Walsh's 1936 *The Virgin and the Swine* languished in obscurity for decades. Only the success of the Ballantine Adult Fantasy Series sparked its rediscovery—after which she completed three more Welsh-legend-inspired books in the same vein in the early 1970s for Ballantine: now rebranded with some success as the *Mabinogion Tetralogy*.

3 Robinson has a codicil to that claim, which helps explain the logic of his own plot rather than character-driven fiction: he argues that science fiction's "ancestry is located in the romance and the tale, rather than in the English domestic novel of character."

4 Le Guin, *The Left Hand of Darkness*, xii.

5 MacDonald, *Phantastes*. Cabell, *Jurgen; a Comedy of Justice*. Manlove, *The Impulse of Fantasy Literature*, 375. Le Guin herself loved MacDonald but notably pushed back against his ponderous moral frameworks: of *The Princess and the Goblin*, "This is a great story, and I love it all, but I love the goblins best" (quoted in Swank, "Ursula's Bookshelf," 152).

6 Manlove, *The Impulse of Fantasy Literature*, 128.

7 Jameson, *Archaeologies of the Future*, 125. It is certainly worth noticing, however, that earlier in the same book Jameson goes out of his way to say that "Le Guin … triumphantly demonstrates that fantasy can also have critical and even demystificatory power" because she "proposes a meditation on magic as such—on its capacities and its existential properties, on a kind of figural mapping of the active and productive subjectivity in its non-alienated state" (66–7).

8 Suvin, "On the Poetics of the Science Fiction Genre," 375.

9 When Jameson comes across fantasy that he deems suitably historically materialist (e.g., works by William Morris and Ursula Le Guin) he rushes to redefine such works (contrary evidence notwithstanding) as science fiction.

10 In previous work I have traced the post-William Morris genealogy of adult prose fantasy up into British "moderate modernism," reading Stella Benson, David Garnett, and Helen Hope Mirrlees (not names to conjure with) alongside Lord Dunsany and Rudyard Kipling's *Puck of Pook's Hill* and *Rewards and Fairies* (Plotz, *Semi-Detached*).

11 Letter to Katharine Tynan on March 14, 1888, Yeats, *The Collected Letters of W. B. Yeats*, I:54–5.

12 Forster, *The Eternal Moment*, 3. It is worth noting that Forster continued to write an immense amount of fiction in his later years that he understood as principally purgative, or expressive of his guiltily suppressed erotic desires. Most he destroyed, but the few works that remain bespeak a continuing attraction to both fantastical and science fictional motifs.

13 Forster, *Where Angels Fear to Tread*, 107.

14 Forster, *Where Angels Fear to Tread*, 158.

15 Forster, *Where Angels Fear to Tread*, 86.

16 Forster, *Where Angels Fear to Tread*, 116.

17 And indeed it is telling that in the section on fantasy in Forster's much later *Aspects of the Novel* he reverts to the figure of the angel, with the same mixture of approbation and hesitation about what it means to introduce an angelic figure (or a figure taken by some characters to be angelic) into a novel:

> We all know that a work of art is an entity, etc. etc.; it has its own laws which are not those of daily life, anything that suits it is true, so why should any question arise about the angel etc. except whether it is suitable to its book? Why place an angel on a different basis from a stockbroker—once in the realm of the fictitious what difference is there between an apparition and a mortgage? I see the soundness of this argument, but my heart refuses to assent. The general tone of novels is so literal that when the fantastic is introduced it produces a special effect.
>
> (Forster, *Aspects of the Novel*, 108)

18 Le Guin, *The Books of Earthsea*, 5, 397.

19 Suvin, "On the Poetics of the Science Fiction Genre." Le Guin's most famous novum, frequently borrowed in later science fiction, was the *ansible*, a faster-than-light radio that enables instantaneous interstellar communication.

20 Jameson's praise for Le Guin's writing as "world reduction" assumes Le Guin's fantasy is best understood, like Robinson's science fiction, as a representation of life on our own earth. That notion makes a mockery of the pride Le Guin takes in conjuring up a world of speaking dragons and power-bearing names. To see Earthsea simply as a

stripped-down Earth ignores Le Guin's aesthetic aim: not to reflect the world as is but to envision life anew, elsewhere. Suvin once wrote, of a collection of critical essays on Le Guin, "I'm sorry that we couldn't find anybody to integrate the Earthsea trilogy with Le Guin's SF" (Suvin, "The Science Fiction of Ursula K. Le Guin," 204). It seems to me that Earthsea's non-integration into an science fiction tradition is exactly what makes it most interesting.

21 O'Brien, *The Third Policeman*, 37.

22 The varieties of fantasy in the last half-century are enormous. Although all fantasy depends on some sort of magical departure from the rules of this world, that does not mean, as readers of Edward Eager and Harry Potter alike will remind you, it is always set off-world. When I interviewed Le Guin she praised "urban fantasy" that drops wizards into downtown Cleveland. By the same token I have always loved Susan Cooper's *Dark Is Rising* series, which drops Arthurian figures into 1970s Britain with some of the same hugger-mugger mashup exuberance as Neil Gaiman's *American Gods*.

23 If you went looking for a nineteenth-century comparison to Delany's vision of fantasy as a space apart from which to look straight back at our own world, laying bare its predictable repetitive flaws, you would certainly find it in Richard Jefferies 1885 *After London*, which imagines terrible natural cataclysm destroying London—only for the same old exploitative history of medieval serfs and lords, of sexism and class-based tyranny, to reassert itself effortlessly. Here comes the New World same as the Old World, might be its refrain. Ditto Delany's. Jefferies, *After London; or, Wild England*.

24 "From Elfland to Poughkeepsie," in Le Guin, *The Language of the Night*, 81.

25 Le Guin, *The Lathe of Heaven*.

Chapter 2

1 Le Guin, *The Books of Earthsea*, 125.

2 Lessing, *The Making of the Representative for Planet 8*; Mitchell, *Cloud Atlas*; Ishiguro, *The Buried Giant*.

3 Book-length studies, from 1976 to the present include: Slusser, *The Farthest Shores of Ursula K. Le Guin*; Spivack, *Ursula K. Le Guin*; Cummins, *Understanding Ursula K. Le Guin*; Rochelle, *Communities of the Heart*;

Burns, *Political Theory, Science Fiction, and Utopian Literature*; Wayne, *Redefining Moral Education*; Lindow, *Dancing the Tao*; Tschachler, *Ursula K. Le Guin*; Seyferth, *Utopie, Anarchismus und Science Fiction*; Cadden, *Ursula K. Le Guin beyond Genre*. There is also a 1983 scholarly bibliography (Cogell, *Ursula K. Le Guin, a Primary and Secondary Bibliography*), a collection of critical essays (Bloom, *Ursula K. Le Guin*), two critical companions (Bernardo and Murphy, *Ursula K. Le Guin* and Reid, *Presenting Ursula K. Le Guin*), as well as a substantial number of books that collect Le Guin's own writing, or interviews with her (Le Guin, *The Language of the Night*; Freedman, *Conversations with Ursula K. Le Guin*; Le Guin, *Ursula K. Le Guin: The Last Interview and Other Conversations*). Recent articles, book chapters, and web pieces, ranging from economic analyses of her utopian thinking to posthumous tributes to a joyful bibliophile and reappraisals of her oeuvre include: Cross, "Naming a Star"; Connolly, *After Human*; Mamola, "Walking towards Elfland"; Roemer, "A Tribute to Ursula K. Le Guin (1929–2018)"; Stone, "The Legacies of Ursula K. Le Guin"; Guynes, "The Ursula K. Le Guin Reread" and many more terrific pieces beyond.

4 Yeats, *Per Amica Silentia Lunae*, 29.

5 In a later afterword to *A Wizard of Earthsea* she specifies both her debt to and her suspicion of the stories she grew up on:

> The conventionality of the story [of A Wizard of Earthsea], and its originality, reflect its existence within and partial subversion of an accepted, recognized tradition, one I grew up with. That is the tradition of fantastic tales and hero stories, which comes down to us like a great river from sources high in the mountains of Myth—a confluence of folk and fairy tale, classical epic, medieval and Renaissance and Eastern romance, romantic ballad, Victorian imaginative tale, and twentieth-century book of fantastic adventure such as T. H. White's Arthurian cycle and Tolkien's great book ... The part of the tradition that I knew best was mostly written (or rewritten for children) in England and northern Europe. The principal characters were men. If the story was heroic, the hero was a white man; most dark-skinned people were inferior or evil.

6 Robinson, "The Realism of our Times."

7 Le Guin, *The Books of Earthsea*, 477.

8 Le Guin, *The Books of Earthsea*, 63.

9 Hence Neil Gaiman's conviction, when he first encountered Earthsea at age eleven, that it contained "a magic of words, a magic of true speaking" (Gaiman, "On Ursula K. Le Guin").

10 Wittgenstein, *Philosophical Investigations*, §19.

11 Le Guin, *The Books of Earthsea*, 855.

12 Delany, *Tales of Nevèrÿon*, 84–5.

13 Le Guin, *The Books of Earthsea*, 740.

14 "From Elfland to Poughkeepsie," in Le Guin, *The Language of the Night*, 81.

15 Le Guin, *The Books of Earthsea*, 7.

16 Laozi, *Tao Te Ching*, 14.

17 Tolkien, *The Monsters and the Critics and Other Essays*, 132.

18 "In human art Fantasy is a thing best left to words, to true literature … Drama [Tolkien probably included film in this category] is naturally hostile to Fantasy. Fantasy, even of the simplest kind, hardly ever succeeds in Drama, when that is presented as it should be, visibly and audibly acted. Fantastic forms are not to be counterfeited. Men dressed up as talking animals may achieve buffoonery or mimicry, but they do not achieve Fantasy" (Tolkien, 142).

19 Le Guin, *The Books of Earthsea*, 239.

20 Le Guin, *The Books of Earthsea*, 240.

21 Weil, *Simone Weil*, 253–4; I am grateful to have been pointed toward Weil's formulation by Moi, "I Came with a Sword."

22 The first phrase is reported by Woodhouse, the second is from an 1817 letter to Benjamin Bailey; Keats, *Selected Letters of John Keats*, 57.

23 Le Guin, *The Books of Earthsea*, 165.

24 Le Guin, *The Books of Earthsea*, 269.

25 Le Guin, *The Books of Earthsea*, 270.

26 Le Guin, *The Books of Earthsea*, 451.

27 Le Guin, *The Books of Earthsea*, 451.

28 Auden, *Collected Poems*, 146–7.

29 Le Guin, *The Books of Earthsea*, 400.

30 Le Guin, *The Books of Earthsea*, 385.

31 J. G. Ballard's 1962 "Which Way to Inner Space" is one early taste of the feverishly experimental air of the 1960s, when writers like Ballard himself, Michael Moorcock, and Philip K. Dick joined Le Guin in breaking all Golden Age norms championed by (among others) the

"Big Three": Robert Heinlein, Isaac Asimov, and Arthur C. Clarke. (Ballard, *A User's Guide to the Millenium: Essays and Reviews*, 195–8.)

32 Brunner, *Stand on Zanzibar*; Ehrlich, *The Population Bomb*.

33 Cf. Thomas Hardy, "Tess's Lament" Verse 6:

> It wears me out to think of it,
> To think of it;
> I cannot bear my fate as writ,
> I'd have my life unbe;
> Would turn my memory to a blot,
> Make every relic of me rot,
> My doings be as they were not,
> And what they've brought to me!

34 For a discussion of decisionism, see Jay, "The Political Existentialism of Hannah Arendt."

35 Sleight, "Scientists and the Bomb."

36 I recently heard Marge Piercy, a celebrated science fiction novelist herself, reflect on why the teenagers of her generation were drawn to the genre "I went to high school in the early '50's and we were all afraid of the atom bomb; we were afraid we're going to die. We needed a way to explore those fears and those dreams. Only science-fiction gave us a place to go to for that" ("Dangerous Visions and New Worlds: Radical Science Fiction 1950 to 1985", Virtual Symposium, February 27, 2022, https://citylights.com/events/dangerous-visions-and-new-worlds-radical-science-fiction-1950-to-1985-day-two/).

37 The similarity between Twain and Le Guin may be most visible in his most fantastical work, *A Connecticut Yankee in King Arthur's Court*. For instance, Twain includes in that book a beautiful little aside about the French Revolution that perfectly aligns with Le Guin's point about the need to step back from our world as it is, to consider underlying truths that we normally blind ourselves to. Twain asks: what is the true cataclysm that the world first recognized in 1789? Not the one we think:

> There were two "Reigns of Terror," if we would but remember it and consider it; the one wrought murder in hot passion, the other in heartless cold blood; the one lasted mere months,

the other had lasted a thousand years; the one inflicted death upon ten thousand persons, the other upon a hundred millions; but our shudders are all for the 'horrors' of the minor Terror, the momentary Terror, so to speak; whereas, what is the horror of swift death by the axe, compared with lifelong death from hunger, cold, insult, cruelty, and heart-break? What is swift death by lightning compared with death by slow fire at the stake? A city cemetery could contain the coffins filled by that brief Terror which we have all been so diligently taught to shiver at and mourn over; but all France could hardly contain the coffins filled by that older and real Terror—that unspeakably bitter and awful Terror which none of us has been taught to see in its vastness or pity as it deserves. (Twain, *Connecticut Yankee in King Arthur's Court*)

38 James, *American Civilization*; James, *Mariners, Renegades, and Castaways: The Story of Herman Melville and the World We Live In*.

39 Plotz, *Semi-Detached*.

40 Samuel Beckett's novels from *Murphy* (1934) onward are shot through with a litany of warning against "the sin of conation": that is to say, to act is to err. But Beckett's comprehensive and deliberately absurdist rejection of activity does not grapple, as Le Guin determinedly does, with the niceties of deciding how to live in the world with that caution about action hanging overhead.

41 Le Guin, *The Books of Earthsea*, 313.

42 "Le Guin, The Story's Where I Go."

43 "Le Guin, The Story's Where I Go."

44 Alex Woloch has an astute discussion of the tension between "character system" and "character space" in realist fiction; Le Guin's preference for story over plot might also be thought of as a preference for "character space" (the messy sense that characters have a life beyond the page) over "character system" (the neat structural logic that says each character is only conjured up by the novelist to solve a particular formal problem (Woloch, *The One vs. the Many*, 15).

45 Kipling, *Kim*.

46 Le Guin, *The Lathe of Heaven*, 63.

47 Delany, *Trouble on Triton: An Ambiguous Heterotopia*; Foucault, "Of Other Spaces: Utopias and Heterotopias."

48 Le Guin, *The Books of Earthsea*, 128–9.

49 "The oft-repeated reproach that Homer is a liar takes nothing from his effectiveness, he does not need to base his story on historical reality, his reality is powerful enough in itself; it ensnares us, weaving its web around us and that suffices him. And this 'real' world into which we are lured exists for itself, contains nothing but itself" (Auerbach, *Mimesis*, 13).

50 "I cordially dislike allegory in all its manifestations, and always have done so since I grew old and wary enough to detect its presence. I much prefer history, true or feigned, with its varied applicability to the thought and experience of readers. I think that many confuse 'applicability' with 'allegory'; but the one resides in the freedom of the reader, and the other in the purposed domination of the author" (Foreword to the second edition, Tolkien, *The Lord of the Rings*).

Chapter 3

1 Le Guin, *The Books of Earthsea*, 559.

2 The core of Le Guin's politics may truly be this refusal of mobilization: her insistence that action is not necessarily better when multiplied by obedience, and that a nation not be conscripted to follow the will or whim of its leader, then it is not *The Dispossessed* but *The Lathe of Heaven* (with its inaction hero George Orr) that propounds her beliefs most clearly. That novel, as it happens, has a Nixon joke woven into it. No matter how much the world gets altered by the meddling Dr. Haber, "Albert M. Merdle was still President of the United States. He, like the shape of continents, appeared to be unchangeable" (Le Guin, *The Lathe of Heaven*, 127). I'd bet my bottom dollar that Merdle (a Dickens character from *Little Dorrit*, but also *little shit*) is Le Guin's avatar for Nixon.

3 Le Guin, *The Books of Earthsea*, 419.

4 Austen, *Pride and Prejudice*, 7.

5 Le Guin, *The Books of Earthsea*, 148–9.

6 Le Guin, *The Books of Earthsea*, 419.

7 In her later "Description of Earthsea" Le Guin helpfully taxonomizes the various categories of male and female magic-users; readers learn that, for example, male sorcerers are in essentially the same position as witches—since they were not educated at Roke, they have a power

that is (or is assumed to be by those who employ them) both weaker and less morally trustworthy than that deployed by an authenticated, staff-bearing Roke wizard. Credentialing is destiny.

8 Eliot, *Middlemarch*, 860.

9 Le Guin, *The Books of Earthsea*, 490.

10 The account I offer here of how aesthetic texts make sense of, confront, and either register or refuse the power of trauma to disrupt narrative orderliness has profited from a vast and divided body of scholarship on that set of questions. Formative texts in that debate include Caruth, *Unclaimed Experience*; Kaplan, *Trauma Culture*; Hirsch, *The Generation of Postmemory*. Especially helpful on the history of trauma's role in literary studies is Leys, *Trauma—a Genealogy*.

11 Darnielle, *Wolf in White Van*, undertakes a similar unpacking of the damaged and twisted life that arises from a single horrific moment. It is especially relevant here because the post-traumatic life the protagonist makes involves creating so persuasive and desolate a dystopic "secondary world" that people who choose to play the game are drawn into it enough that they start believing in its real-world existence, thus triggering another traumatic event.

12 Le Guin, *The Books of Earthsea*, 500.

13 Arendt, *The Human Condition*, 157, quoting Isak Dinesen.

14 Le Guin, *The Books of Earthsea*, 518.

15 In our interview, Le Guin spoke eloquently about her attachment to the past tense as a novelist's necessity, and her unease with contemporary fiction narrated only in the present.

16 Yeats, *The Poems*, 181.

17 Cf. a recent critique of novels that embrace trauma at the expense of narrative momentum (Sehgal, "The Case against the Trauma Plot").

18 Le Guin, *The Books of Earthsea*, 990.

19 Scarry, *The Body in Pain*.

20 In *The Other Wind* the same pattern arises when the question of "cheating death" returns as an existential question. Those who practice the spell magic of Earthsea, with its true names, have consigned their dead to an eternity living on as souls without bodies. On the other hand, dragons, animals, and humans like the Kargads, (who do not practice that magic) are able to live a bodily life and then die completely, so that their souls and bodies both rejoin the universe to be reassembled into other beings.

21 Le Guin, *The Books of Earthsea*, 490.
22 Arendt, *The Human Condition*. "It is true that totalitarian domination tried to establish these holes of oblivion into which all deeds, good and evil, would disappear, but just as the Nazis' feverish attempts, from June, 1942 on, to erase all traces of the massacres—through cremation, through burning in open pits, through the use of explosives and flame-throwers and bone-crushing machinery—were doomed to failure, so all efforts to let their opponents 'disappear in silent anonymity' were in vain. The holes of oblivion do not exist. Nothing human is that perfect, and there are simply too many people in the world to make oblivion possible. One man will always be left alive to tell the story. Hence, nothing can ever be 'practically useless,' at least, not in the long run" (Arendt, *Eichmann in Jerusalem: A Report on the Banality of Evil*, 109).
23 Vonnegut, *Slaughterhouse-Five*, 28.
24 Le Guin, *The Books of Earthsea*, 674.
25 Randall Jarrell has a line that paraphrases what some of the human residents of Earthsea think about dragons: "All that I've never thought of, think of me!" ("A Sick Child" in Jarrell, *The Complete Poems*).
26 Le Guin, *The Books of Earthsea*, 828.
27 Le Guin, *The Books of Earthsea*, 803.
28 Le Guin, "Why Are Americans Afraid of Dragons?" 40.
29 Le Guin, *The Books of Earthsea*, 466–7.
30 I learned about the passage in Davis, *Ornamental Aesthetics*, 86. A wonderful book.
31 In Marlowe's *Faustus*, Mephistopheles puts the idea slightly differently: "Why this is hell, nor am I out of it."
32 Graeber and Wengrow, *The Dawn of Everything*.
33 Abbott, Lindgren, and Banchoff, *Flatland*.
34 Wharton, *The House of Mirth*, 276.
35 Goffman, *The Presentation of Self in Everyday Life*.
36 Arendt, *Lectures on Kant's Political Philosophy*, 43.
37 Benjamin, "Left-Wing Melancholy (On Erich Kästner's New Book of Poems)."
38 Hardy and also Gillian Beer ghost plots.
39 There is an echo of the Ariadne story in *Tombs of Atuan*: the girl in the maze with the shining thread to lead Theseus out. However there is a difference: Ariadne ends up a forgotten side-plot in the Greek myth, quickly consigned to another island as Theseus wends his triumphant

way home. This Ariadne, by contrast, remains center of her own story, which takes her beyond the triumphant return to Havnor.

40 Alder's vocation strikes me as a sly reference to Le Guin's old and dear friend, Philip K. Dick. His often-overlooked *Galactic Pot-Healer* (1969) has some of the same loopy inventiveness that inspired Le Guin to write world-altering dreams into *The Lathe of Heaven*. When I spoke with Le Guin she called that novel her tribute to Dick; I suspect that Alder may be another.

41 Howard Norman, personal communication, September, 2021.

Chapter 4

1 Le Guin, *The Books of Earthsea*, 984–5.
2 Conrad, *Heart of Darkness*, 87.
3 Eliot, *Middlemarch*, 999.
4 I think it was Marshall McLuhan who wrote "Given TV's awesome powers to educate—aren't you grateful it doesn't?" A very George Orr sentiment.
5 Years later, my friend Ivan Kreilkamp, also the son of an English professor, thought of the perfect title for the book that could be written about us Gen X-ers who were more or less the first American men ever to follow their mothers into their profession: *Momma's Boys*.
6 When the O. J. Simpson verdict was announced I was eating lunch with him in the basement of the faculty club. As I stumblingly tried to explain the fuss, it finally dawned on me that he had no idea who O. J. was and that football itself was only a dim fact on his horizon.
7 "Afterwards," in Hardy, *Thomas Hardy*, 356.
8 Plotz, "Beverly Cleary Forever (1916–2021)."
9 Orwell, *The Road to Wigan Pier*, 85.
10 Judith A. Plotz, *Romanticism and the Vocation of Childhood*; Helen Plotz, *Gladly Learn and Gladly Teach*; Helen Plotz, *Untune the Sky: Poems of Music and the Dance*; Helen Plotz, *Imagination's Other Place: Poems of Science and Mathematics*.
11 A line from "The Dry Salvages" in Eliot, *Collected Poems 1909–1962*, 206.
12 If that love were not obvious from Le Guin's writing, I know because I brought her a print of William Morris as a present, and her whole face lit up.
13 Morris, *A Dream of John Ball*.

14 Price, "Reader's Block."

15 Le Guin, *The Books of Earthsea*, 559.

16 Young-Bruehl, *Hannah Arendt: For Love of the World*.

17 Le Guin, *The Books of Earthsea*, 984.

18 of Samosata, *Selected Works*, 220.

19 "Gender is a kind of imitation for which there is no original; in fact, it is a kind of imitation that produces the very notion of the original as an effect and consequence of the imitation itself … gay identities work neither to copy nor emulate heterosexuality, but rather, to expose heterosexuality as an incessant and panicked imitation of its own naturalized idealization. That heterosexuality is always in the act of elaborating itself is evidence that it is perpetually at risk" (Butler, "Imitation and Gender Insubordination," 313).

20 Steven Justice's 2008 "Did the Middle Ages Believe their Own Miracles?" showed me that even in an avowedly highly religious, highly churched era, religious thinkers clearly distinguished between known facts—sunrise, sunset, death—and miracles, impossible and hence requiring to be actively *believed in* rather than simply accepted ("medieval sources not only anticipate modern accounts of their belief but suppose a conceptually more supple and forceful account of their own"). Faith is not knowledge, belief is not knowing. The significance of "I believe *because* it is impossible" finally registered for me (Justice, "Did the Middle Ages Believe in Their Miracles?").

WORKS CITED

Abbott, Edwin Abbott, William F. Lindgren, and Thomas Banchoff. *Flatland: An Edition with Notes and Commentary*. Cambridge; New York: Washington, DC: Cambridge University Press; Mathematical Association of America, 2010.

Arendt, Hannah. *Eichmann in Jerusalem: A Report on the Banality of Evil*. New York: Viking Press, 1963.

Arendt, Hannah. *Lectures on Kant's Political Philosophy*. Edited by Ronald Beiner. Chicago: University of Chicago Press, 1982.

Arendt, Hannah. *The Human Condition*. Second edition. Introduction by Margaret Canovan. Chicago: University of Chicago Press, 1998.

Auden, W. H. *Collected Poems*. London: Faber & Faber, 1976.

Auerbach, Erich. *Mimesis: The Representation of Reality in Western Literature*. Edited by Jan M. Ziolkowski. Fiftieth anniversary edition. Princeton, NJ: Princeton University Press, 2003.

Austen, Jane. *Pride and Prejudice*. Oxford World's Classics (Oxford University Press). Oxford [England]; New York: Oxford University Press, 1999.

Ballard, J. G. *A User's Guide to the Millenium: Essays and Reviews*. London: Flamingo, 1997.

Benjamin, Walter. "Left-Wing Melancholy (On Erich Kästner's New Book of Poems)." *Screen* 15, no. 2 (July 1, 1974): 28–32. https://doi.org/10.1093/screen/15.2.28.

Bernardo, Susan M., and Graham J. Murphy. *Ursula K. Le Guin: A Critical Companion*. Critical Companions to Popular Contemporary Writers. Westport, CT: Greenwood Press, 2006.

Bloom, Harold, ed. *Ursula K. Le Guin*. Modern Critical Views. New York: Chelsea House Publishers, 1986.

Brunner, John. *Stand on Zanzibar*. Garden City, New York: Doubleday & Company, 1968.

Burns, Tony. *Political Theory, Science Fiction, and Utopian Literature: Ursula K. Le Guin and* The Dispossessed. Lanham, MD: Rowman & Littlefield, 2008.

Butler, Judith. "Imitation and Gender Insubordination." In Lesbian and Gay Studies Reader, edited by Henry Abelove, Michèle Aina Barale, and David M. Halperin, 307–20. New York: Routledge, 1993.

Cabell, James Branch. *Jurgen: A Comedy of Justice.* New York: McBride & Company, 1928.

Cadden, Michael. *Ursula K. Le Guin beyond Genre: Fiction for Children and Adults.* Children's Literature and Culture; v. 33. New York: Routledge, 2005.

Caruth, Cathy. *Unclaimed Experience: Trauma, Narrative, and History.* Twentieth anniversary edition. Baltimore, MD: Johns Hopkins University Press, 2016.

Cather, Willa. "The Novel Démeublé." The New Republic 30 (April 12, 1922): 5–6.

Cogell, Elizabeth Cummins. *Ursula K. Le Guin: A Primary and Secondary Bibliography.* Masters of Science Fiction and Fantasy. Boston, MA: G. K. Hall, 1983.

Connolly, Thomas. *After Human: A Critical History of the Human in Science Fiction from Shelley to Le Guin.* Liverpool: Liverpool University Press, 2021.

Conrad, Joseph. *Heart of Darkness: Authoritative Text, Backgrounds and Contexts, Criticism.* Fourth edition. Norton Critical Edition. New York: Norton, 2006.

Cooper, Susan, The Dark is Rising. New York: Aladdin, 1973.

Cross, Katherine. "Naming a Star: Ursula Le Guin's *The Dispossessed* and the Reimagining of Utopianism." *The American Journal of Economics and Sociology* 77, no. 5 (2018): 1329–52.

Cummins, Elizabeth. *Understanding Ursula K. Le Guin.* Columbia, SC: University of South Carolina Press, 1990.

Darnielle, John. *Wolf in White Van.* New York: Farrar, Straus and Giroux, 2014.

Davis, Theo. *Ornamental Aesthetics: The Poetry of Attending in Thoreau, Dickinson, and Whitman.* New York: Oxford University Press, 2016.

Delany, Samuel R. *Tales of Nevèrÿon.* Hanover, NH: University Press of New England for Wesleyan University Press, 1993.

Delany, Samuel R. *Trouble on Triton: An Ambiguous Heterotopia.* Middletown, CT: Wesleyan University Press, 1996.

Dick, Philip K. *Galactic Pot-Healer.* New York: Berkley Publishing Corporation, 1969.

Ehrlich, Paul R. *The Population Bomb.* New York: Ballantine Books, 1968.

Eliot, George. *Middlemarch*. Oxford: Oxford University Press, 2019.

Eliot, T. S. *Collected Poems 1909–1962*. Cambridge: Chadwyck-Healey, 1999.

Forster, E. M. *Where Angels Fear to Tread*. New York: Knopf, 1920.

Forster, E. M. *Aspects of the Novel*. New York: Harcourt, Brace & Company, 1927.

Forster, E. M. *The Eternal Moment and Other Stories*. New York: Harcourt, Brace & Company, 1928.

Foucault, Michel. "Of Other Spaces: Utopias and Heterotopias." *Architecture/Mouvement/Continuitie*, October 1984.

Freedman, Carl Howard, ed. *Conversations with Ursula K. Le Guin*. Literary Conversations Series. Jackson, MS: University Press of Mississippi, 2008.

Gaiman, Neil. *American Gods: A Novel*. New York: W. Morrow, 2001.

Gaiman, Neil. "On Ursula K. Le Guin." Accessed October 26, 2021. https://www.loa.org/news-and-views/1372-neil-gaiman-on-ursula-k-le-guin-a-magic-of-true-speaking.

Goffman, Erving. *The Presentation of Self in Everyday Life*. Woodstock, NY: Overlook Press, 1973.

Graeber, David, and D. Wengrow. *The Dawn of Everything: A New History of Humanity*. New York: Farrar, Straus and Giroux, 2021.

Guynes, Sean. "The Ursula K. Le Guin Reread." Tor.com. Accessed August 25, 2021. https://www.tor.com/series/the-ursula-k-le-guin-reread/.

Hardy, Thomas. *Thomas Hardy: The Complete Poems*. Houndmills, Basingstoke; New York: Palgrave, 2001.

Hirsch, Marianne. *The Generation of Postmemory: Writing and Visual Culture after the Holocaust*. Gender and Culture. New York: Columbia University Press, 2012.

Ishiguro, Kazuo. *The Buried Giant*. New York: Alfred A. Knopf, 2015.

James, C. L. R. *Mariners, Renegades, and Castaways: The Story of Herman Melville and the World We Live In*. New York:, 1953.

James, C. L. R. (Cyril Lionel Robert). *American Civilization*. Cambridge, MA: Blackwell, 1993.

Jameson, Fredric. *Archaeologies of the Future: The Desire Called Utopia and Other Science Fictions*. London; New York: Verso, 2005.

Jarrell, Randall. *The Complete Poems*. New York: Noonday Press, 1996.

Jay, Martin. "The Political Existentialism of Hannah Arendt." In *Permanent Exiles: Essays on the Intellectual Migration from Germany to America*, 237–56. New York: Columbia University Press, 1986.

Jefferies, Richard. *After London; or, Wild England*. London, New York: Cassell & Company, 1885.

Justice, Steven. "Did the Middle Ages Believe in their Miracles?" *Representations* 103, no. 1 (2008): 1–29.

Kaplan, E. Ann. *Trauma Culture: The Politics of Terror and Loss in Media and Literature*. New Brunswick, NJ: Rutgers University Press, 2005.

Keats, John. *Selected Letters of John Keats*. Revised edition. Cambridge, MA: Harvard University Press, 2002.

Kipling, Rudyard. *Kim*. Penguin Twentieth-Century Classics. New York, London: Penguin Books, 1989.

Kroeber, Theodora. *Ishi in Two Worlds: A Biography of the Last Wild Indian in North America*. Berkeley, CA: University of California Press, 1969.

Laozi. *Tao Te Ching: A Book about the Way and the Power of the Way*. Translated by Ursula K. Le Guin. Boston: Shambhala, 1997.

Le Guin, Ursula K. *The Lathe of Heaven*. New York: C. Scribner's Sons, 1971.

Le Guin, Ursula K. *The New Atlantis and Other Novellas of Science Fiction*. Edited by Gene Wolfe. New York: Hawthorn Books, 1975.

Le Guin, Ursula K. "Why Are Americans Afraid of Dragons?" 39–45 In *The Language of the Night*. Harper, 1979.

Le Guin, Ursula K. *The Beginning Place*. New York: Harper & Row, 1980.

Le Guin, Ursula K. *The Language of the Night: Essays on Fantasy and Science Fiction*. Edited and with Introductions by Susan Wood. New York: Berkley Books, 1982.

Le Guin, Ursula K. *The Left Hand of Darkness*. Fiftieth anniversary edition. New York: Ace Books, 1987.

Le Guin, Ursula K. *The Dispossessed*. New York, NY: Harper Voyager, 1994.

Le Guin, Ursula K. *The Lathe of Heaven*. New York: Scribner, 2008.

Le Guin, Ursula K. "The Story's Where I Go." Interview by John Plotz, June 15, 2015. https://www.publicbooks.org/the-storys-where-i-go-an-interview-with-ursula-k-le-guin/.

Le Guin, Ursula K. *The Books of Earthsea: The Complete Illustrated Edition*. First Saga edition. New York: Saga Press, 2018.

Le Guin, Ursula K. *Ursula K. Le Guin: The Last Interview and Other Conversations*. Last Interview Series. Brooklyn; London: Melville House, 2019.

Le Guin, Ursula K. "Acceptance Speech—The National Book Foundation Medal for Distinguished Contribution to American Letters." Accessed October 28, 2021. https://www.ursulakleguin.com/nbf-medal.

Lessing, Doris. *The Making of the Representative for Planet 8*. Canopus in Argos Archives. New York: Knopf, 1982.

Leys, Ruth. *Trauma: A Genealogy*. Chicago, IL: University of Chicago Press, 2003.

Lindow, Sandra J. *Dancing the Tao: Le Guin and Moral Development*. Newcastle-upon-Tyne: Cambridge Scholars Publisher, 2012.

MacDonald, George. *Phantastes: A Faerie Romance for Men and Women*. London: Smith, Elder, 1858.

MacDonald, George. *The Princess and the Goblin*. New York: The Macmillan Company, 1926.

Mamola, Gabriel. "Walking towards Elfland: Fantasy and Utopia in Ursula K. Le Guin's *The Ones Who Walk Away from Omelas*." *Extrapolation* 59, no. 2 (2018): 149–62.

Manlove, C. N. *The Impulse of Fantasy Literature*. Kent, OH: Kent State University Press, 1983.

Mendlesohn, Farah. *Rhetorics of Fantasy*. Middletown, CT: Wesleyan University Press, 2008.

Milton, John. *Paradise Lost*. Edited by Stephen B. Dobranski. New York, N.Y.: W.W. Norton & Company, Inc., 2022.

Mitchell, David. *Cloud Atlas*. New York: Random House Trade Paperbacks, 2004.

Moi, Toril. Review of *I Came with a Sword*, by Robert Zaretsky. London Review of Books, July 1, 2021.

Morris, William. *A Dream of John Ball*, 1888. https://www.marxists.org/archive/morris/works/1886/johnball/chapters/chapter4.htm.

O'Brien, Flann. *The Third Policeman*. John F. Byrne Irish Literature Series. Normal, IL: Dalkey Archive Press, 1999.

Orwell, George. *The Road to Wigan Pier*. London: Victor Gollancz, 1937.

Plotz, Helen. *Imagination's Other Place: Poems of Science and Mathematics*. New York: Crowell, 1955.

Plotz, Helen. *Untune the Sky: Poems of Music and the Dance*. New York: Crowell, 1957.

Plotz, Helen. *Gladly Learn and Gladly Teach: Poems of the School Experience*. First edition. New York: Greenwillow Books, 1981.

Plotz, John. "Le Guin's Anarchist Aesthetics." *Public Books*, October 15, 2015. http://www.publicbooks.org/fiction/le-guins-anarchist-aesthetics.

Plotz, John. *Semi-Detached: The Aesthetics of Virtual Experience since Dickens*. Princeton: Princeton University Press, 2017.

Plotz, John. "Beverly Cleary Forever (1916–2021)." *Public Books*, April 12, 2021. https://www.publicbooks.org/beverly-cleary-forever-1916-2021/.

Plotz, Judith A. *Romanticism and the Vocation of Childhood*. New York: Palgrave, 2001.

Price, Leah. "Reader's Block." *Victorian Studies* 46, no. 2 (2004): 231–42.

Reid, Suzanne Elizabeth. *Presenting Ursula K. Le Guin*. New York; London: Twayne Publishers; Prentice Hall International, 1997.

Rilke, Rainer Maria. *Ahead of All Parting: The Selected Poetry and Prose of Rainer Maria Rilke*. Translated by Stephen Mitchell. Westminster: Random House, 2015.

Robinson, Kim Stanley. "The Realism of Our Times: Kim Stanley Robinson on How Science Fiction Works." Interview by John Plotz, September 23, 2020. https://www.publicbooks.org/the-realism-of-our-times-kim-stanley-robinson-on-how-science-fiction-works/.

Rochelle, Warren. *Communities of the Heart: The Rhetoric of Myth in the Fiction of Ursula K. Le Guin*. Liverpool Science Fiction Texts and Studies. Liverpool: Liverpool University Press, 2001.

Roemer, Kenneth M. "A Tribute to Ursula K. Le Guin (1929–2018)." *Utopian Studies* 29, no. 2 (2018): 117–26.

Samosata, Lucian of. *Selected Works*. Indianapolis: Bobbs-Merrill, 1965.

Scarry, Elaine. *The Body in Pain: The Making and Unmaking of the World*. New York: Oxford University Press, 1985.

Sehgal, Parul. "The Case against the Trauma Plot." The New Yorker, December 27, 2021. https://www.newyorker.com/magazine/2022/01/03/the-case-against-the-trauma-plot.

Seyferth, Peter. *Utopie, Anarchismus und Science Fiction: Ursula K. Le Guins Werke von 1962 bis 2002*. Politica et Ars; Bd. 16. Berlin: Lit, 2008.

Sleight, Jessica. "Scientists and the Bomb: 'The Destroyer of Worlds.'" *Global Zero*, July 25, 2019. https://www.globalzero.org/updates/scientists-and-the-bomb-the-destroyer-of-worlds/.

Slusser, George Edgar. *The Farthest Shores of Ursula K. Le Guin*. Popular Writers of Today; v. 3. San Bernardino, CA: Borgo Press, 1976.

Spivack, Charlotte. *Ursula K. Le Guin*. Boston, MA: Twayne Publishers, 1984.

Stone, Katie. "The Legacies of Ursula K. Le Guin: Science, Fiction, and Ethics for the Anthropocene." *Utopian Studies* 31, no. 1 (2020): 227–33.

Suvin, Darko. "On the Poetics of the Science Fiction Genre." *College English* 34, no. 3 (1972): 372–82. https://doi.org/10.2307/375141.

Suvin, Darko. "The Science Fiction of Ursula K. Le Guin." *Science-Fiction Studies* 2 (1975): 203–204.

Swank, Kris. "Ursula's Bookshelf." *Mythlore: A Journal of J.R.R. Tolkien, C.S. Lewis, Charles Williams, and Mythopoeic Literature* 39, no. 2 (April 23, 2021) 137–155.

Tolkien, J. R. R. *The Lord of the Rings*. Second edition. London: Allen & Unwin, 1966.

Tolkien, J. R. R. *The Monsters and the Critics and Other Essays*. Edited by Christopher Tolkien. London: HarperCollins, 1997.

Tschachler, Heinz. *Ursula K. Le Guin*. Boise State University Western Writers Series No. 148. Boise, ID: Boise State University, 2001.

Twain, Mark. *Connecticut Yankee in King Arthur's Court*. Edited by Bernard L. Stein. Mark Twain Library. Berkeley, CA: University of California Press, 2014.

Vonnegut, Kurt. *Slaughterhouse-Five: Or, The Children's Crusade, a Duty-Dance with Death*. New York: Delacorte Press, 1969.

Walton, Evangeline. *The Virgin and the Swine: The Fourth Branch of the Mabinogi*. Chicago; New York: Willett, Clark & Co., 1936.

Wayne, Kathryn Ross. *Redefining Moral Education: Life, Le Guin, and Language*. San Francisco, CA: Austin & Winfield, 1996.

Weil, Simone. *Simone Weil: An Anthology*. London; New York: Penguin, 2005.

Wharton, Edith. *The House of Mirth*. Hudson River Editions. New York: Scribner's, 1975.

Williamson, Jamie. *The Evolution of Modern Fantasy: From Antiquarianism to the Ballantine Adult Fantasy Series*. First edition. New York: Palgrave Macmillan, 2015.

Wittgenstein, Ludwig. *Philosophical Investigations*. Oxford: Blackwell, 2001.

Woloch, Alex. *The One vs. the Many: Minor Characters and the Space of the Protagonist in the Novel*. Course Book. Princeton, NJ: Princeton University Press, 2004.

Yeats, W. B. *Per Amica Silentia Lunae*. New York: Macmillan, 1918.

Yeats, W. B. *The Collected Letters of W. B. Yeats*. Oxford; New York: Clarendon Press, 1986.

Yeats, W. B. *The Poems*. Revised edition. New York: Macmillan, 1989.

Young-Bruehl, Elisabeth. *Hannah Arendt: For Love of the World*. New Haven, CT: Yale University Press, 1982.

INDEX

Please note that titles by Le Guin are followed by dates in parentheses.